The Ultimate Success Secret

Build the Orthodontic Practice of Your Dreams

Dustin S. Burleson
Dan S. Kennedy

Burleson Media Group

Kansas City, Missouri

CONTENTS

To those who aggressively yearn for rational and accurate ideas, concepts and strategies and ruthlessly seek and implement them with irrational and unorthodox vigor.

Strength and growth come only through continuous effort and struggle.

NAPOLEON HILL

[1]

Take Action to Escape from Prison

Dan S. Kennedy

HAVE YOU EVER been inside a real prison? A friend of mine, some years ago, served one year in the Ohio State Penitentiary, and I went to visit him frequently. I can tell you: nothing you see on TV or in the movies can even half prepare you for the shock of the real thing. I don't remember how many times I went inside and back out from behind those prison walls, but the awe, fear, disability, and depression I felt never lessened from the first time to the last. No description I could write could convey the powerlessness that came over me in that environment. There are millions of people enduring that environment every day.

But that's a small number compared to the many millions of people who might as well be in such a prison for the little joy and satisfaction they're deriving from life. People build their own prisons, incarcerate themselves in them, and make the environments every bit as bleak, stark, depressing, and debilitating as the actual penitentiary I visited in Ohio. These people's private prisons' block walls are constructed of complaints and resentments, the mortar from excuses, the bars forged from pessimism and procrastination.

We might say that they are locked up in "Pity Prison." Their sentence is indefinite and of their own making. They could walk out as a free man or woman at any time – if they would just apply The Ultimate Secret of Success.

A WORD ABOUT HEROES

As I finished the first edition of this book, the O.J. Simpson trial had sparked a national discussion of the relative wisdom or lack thereof of turning sports champions, entertainers, and other public celebrities into heroic role models. NBA star Charles Barkley publicly insisted, "Athletes are not role models." Unfortunately, we cannot discourage countless young people from giving them hero status. The argument against viewing people as heroes based on their proclivity for making baskets, catching passes, packing concert halls, or delivering lines in movies is a good one, as too many seem to have an equal proclivity for squandering their status, money, and time on drugs, alcohol, epic sexual misbehavior, and violence.

Actually, there are plenty of *real* heroes all around us. Once, while killing time at the airport, I got my shoes shined. The lady doing the job, I'd guess about 35 or 36 years old, was finishing her second shift of the day with me, at 6:00 PM. Just as she was finishing, the pay phone rang; as it turns out, her teenage daughter and son were required to call her every hour to check in. She was a divorced mother of two, a high school grad, with very limited marketable job skills, doing a relatively tough job. Her compensation depended on tips, so the quality of her work, her attitude, and her smile were critical; she was raising two teenagers; and she was saving up money to go back to school. I had to inquire and prod to find all this out. She was not complaining, not whining, not looking for pity. A real hero.

After a speaking engagement in Harrisburg, Pennsylvania, I was eating dinner in the Holiday Inn restaurant. Seated several tables away, alone, was a man about my age, in a wheelchair. His hands were apparently of little use to him. He dined on a bowl of soup and a soft drink, both consumed through a straw. When the check was brought to him, he somehow produced his wallet – I didn't see how – and extracted dollar bills from it with his teeth. Here was a man saddled with obvious shoulder-to-toes physical disabilities that made a simple journey to a restaurant difficult, tiring, possibly embarrassing. No one would criticize him for dropping out and copping out. But he refused to let his handicaps imprison him. A real hero.

During a weekend in Las Vegas, I was leaving Caesars Palace. The man getting his car from the valet ahead of me was also in a wheelchair. He and the valet knew each other and joked together as the man hoisted himself from his wheelchair into the car. The valet then left to retrieve my car. I walked over and asked the man if he would like help getting his wheelchair into his car. "Thanks," he said, "but it's not necessary. I've been doing this for myself for 30 years and I'm thankful that I can." One-handed, he folded up the wheelchair, pulled it into the car behind him, slid across the seat, and drove off. He, too, refused to be imprisoned by his handicap. A real hero.

I had reason to recall these instances and individuals, when my Dad had a re-occurrence of an unusual neurological condition that put him flat on his back in the hospital, unable to sit up by himself, feed himself, stand, walk, or do much of anything else. His doctors did their best to convince him that he, at best, might not go beyond being helped into a wheelchair. He set goals for regaining leg strength and balance. Then for control of the upper body. Then for feeding himself. Then for dressing himself. Then he moved from hospital to long-term care facility, today's euphemism for nursing home. Then he set goals for walking. And finally he got into his own car and drove himself to his apartment. Then he came back to work at the office.

I once had a blind man in a sales organization I managed. He had not been blind at birth but had lost his sight in his late teens. He worked with his wife in our business, and he was an enthusiastic, effective salesperson. He told me a favorite pastime was washing and waxing his car at ten or eleven o'clock at night, in the dark; it didn't matter to him but it sure bugged his neighbors! I asked him how it was that he had avoided bitterness or self-pity. He told me: "very early on, I got to meet and talk with many other blind people and I realized that many had let their lack of sight ruin their lives. They built little prisons for themselves and locked themselves in. I was determined not to do that." A real hero.

Each of these individuals' lives demonstrates that positive attitudes and actions, even in the most negative of circumstances, can make a big difference.

WHO ELSE IS AFRAID OF PUBLIC S-S-S-SPEAKING?

Phobias are real. I've had the privilege of working with Florence Henderson on a couple of TV projects, and gotten to know her. Did you know that, following the cancellation of "The Brady Bunch," her career dried up, and her fear of flying rose up and dominated her, crippling her pursuit of career opportunities, because she could not get on an airplane? Barbara Streisand stopped doing concerts thanks to uncontrollable stage freight. Johnny Carson reportedly suffered from incredible anxiety before every show. A comedian I know well, who I won't name, has such severe stage fright that he vomits before most performances.

But there's not a phobia on earth that can't be treated, conquered, controlled.

Who's afraid of speaking in public? Just about everybody! Several surveys have shown that more people fear public speaking than fear heights, snakes, serious illness, accidental death, or financial failure. One survey of Fortune 1000 executives revealed speaking to groups as their #1 fear. I've been fortunate to earn a large income from speaking; as my career progressed, from a few thousand dollars to $50,000.00 and up from each speech. But if you went back to the time in my childhood when I stuttered almost uncontrollably – when I could turn one short sentence into one long s-s-s-s-s-seminar – who would have predicted this career for me?

Although the problem lessened as I matured, to this day I am still at risk of getting hung up on a word, starting to stutter, embarrassing myself on stage, on the phone, or in conversation. Was it smart to choose careers in selling and speaking? Who would have blamed me for letting this influence my career choices? I refused to do that.

My friends John and Greg Rice were imprisoned by their midget size, until a man by the name of Glenn Turner ("Dare To Be Great") got a hold of them. John and Greg can't reach all the elevator buttons without something to stand on, and Glenn Turner was the first person to tell them that even "little men" could do big things. John and Greg have become very popular motivational speakers, on the subject of Thinking Big! – even though they have to climb up onto a table so the audience can see them.

They achieved considerable success as real estate salesmen, even though they had to ask their customers to describe the things above sink level that they couldn't see. They've been featured on countless TV programs and in movies, built a sizable real estate investment business, and live a top quality lifestyle in sunny Florida.

FOR EVERY HANDICAP, OBSTACLE AND TRAGEDY, THERE ARE TWO STORIES

Go ahead, name a handicap. Born and raised in a ghetto, as a latch-key kid, then surrounded by gangs, crime, drugs. A physical handicap. A crippling accident. A terrible disease. Illiteracy. Lack of education. A speech impediment. Severe phobia. Name the handicap. There are two stories to be found for every one you can think of. Story #1, unfortunately the most common, will be of people who've let that handicap imprison them. Story #2 will be of the person who has accomplished the most extraordinary things in spite of, in some cases because of, that very same handicap. Each individual, by his or her actions, chooses which story will be theirs.

IMPRISONING	THE ACTION MODEL
I can't	I will
Resentment	Gratitude
Desire for sympathy	Desire for accomplishment
Dwelling on "It's not fair"	Search for opportunities
Acceptance	Invention
"Maybe tomorrow…"	Do it now!
Withdrawal	Participation
Depression	Celebration of even small victories

"It's an impossible situation, but it has possibilities!" – Sam Goldwyn

[2]

From Personal Prison to Practice Freedom

Dustin S. Burleson

MANY DOCTORS SPEND their entire careers just waiting for something to happen. Day in and day out, they go through the motions, not all that happy with the results. Yet they are not taking action in order to make things happen. Years ago, I asked myself whether I wanted to be that kind of doctor and have that type of practice, or whether I wanted to be someone who gets things done and makes things happen. The bottom line, which many doctors in business do not seem to realize, is that they have to take action in order to make things happen. Success doesn't just come to you as you sit by idly, waiting. Not even if you cross your fingers!

When was the last time you got excited about your accomplishments toward your personal goals? Can you feel yourself making big strides toward an inspiring outcome? If not, why? If not now, when? I recently read the book *Action! Nothing Happens Until Something Moves*, by Robert Ringer. It's a great book that makes a lot of sense. The author lays out the need for people to be proactive in making things happen. Smart doctors take personal action if they want their lives to move forward. It all comes down to knowing what you want out of life, having a clear vision for your future, and then taking the steps or actions necessary to make it happen. Unfortunately, I see far too many clients who have been sitting in practices with no vision, who lack a strategy for growth, and lead uninspired teams through the clinical drudgery of private practice, working with patients who are only interested in the cheapest price or what their insurance will pay for. This doesn't sound like private practice. It sounds like a personal prison to me.

> *Contrary to popular belief, you don't need to be motivated to act. If necessary, force yourself to take action and motivation will follow."*
> *– Robert Ringer*

Getting Started on Your Journey

To make the right things happen in my practice, I first had to discover where I wanted to go. Consider how odd it would be if you spent the morning packing your suitcases to take a trip, loaded them into the car, put a stop on the newspaper delivery, filled up the gas tank, and then headed down the road...only then realizing that you had no map, and no destination in mind. You hadn't actually thought about where you were going. You did everything right, leading up to the trip, making sure you were well packed and ready to go, but because you didn't decide *where* to go, there is a good chance you may not be all that thrilled with where you end up.

Perhaps, along the way, you decide to try blindly turning this way and that way, just hoping that something great will happen. For a few people, it just may, if they get lucky. But odds are good that those who have taken the time to plan out their journey and determine their destination are going to be much happier, not only with the ride, but also with the outcome when they finally arrive.

Luck is what happens when preparation meets opportunity." – Seneca

Your practice is much like taking a trip. You did everything right in becoming a doctor and learning your craft. But if you don't have a vision for what you want, and don't choose the right route to get there, you will probably be sorely disappointed with both the journey and the destination. Again, nothing is going to happen until something moves. And the something that needs to move is you and your preconceived notions about how your business operates.

Another way of looking at this is parachuting. When you go parachuting, you pack your own chute. By doing this, you know that everything is packed and organized correctly. Even if you haven't packed your own chute, there is a good chance you are going to take a few moments to double-check someone else's handiwork. You want to make sure that everything is okay so that you are assured of a safe landing. Your chute is in your own hands, so it is safe to say that if you are in trouble once you get going, there is a good chance that it is a problem of your own making. In your business, if you feel – like so many other doctors – that you are a prisoner, then there is a good chance that your confinement is of your own making. From coast to coast, doctors fly to Kansas City and pay me large sums to solve their "practice problems." What I have discovered is that many of the problems in private practice fall into the category of personal prisons. Marketing miracles, staff turnarounds, fee restructuring, scheduling templates, and improved public relations are frequently helpful but never the primary problem. The primary problem for so many doctors is their inability to see the personal prisons they have built around themselves:

> "My patients just don't value quality care; my city is too big with too many competitors; my city is too small; my patients only want what insurance will pay for; my patients are too busy and never keep their appointments; my staff just won't take ownership of the practice; my associates don't understand what it takes to run this place; my staff is too lazy; my staff is too young; my staff is too old; we have tried everything and nothing works in my town; my town is different; my patients are different; my staff is different; but I'm a specialist; but I'm a generalist; you just don't understand."

You are packing your own parachute. Smart doctors pack the chute correctly, doing what needs to be done, and being proactive. This is no time to sit on the sidelines, hoping someone else comes to your rescue. Get off the bench and get actively involved in creating your future. That is the only way to ensure the best possible outcome.

"The best way to predict your future is to create it." – Peter Drucker

Success Leaves Clues

Take a look around your town. (Okay, you don't have to physically get up and go look around, but figuratively speaking.) Is there someone in your town or nearby that is successfully doing what you want to do? Try to identify who that is. Then, start emulating that person. As much as possible, study their actions. Carry out some online research about their practice to see what they are doing. Read the feedback their patients are giving in reviews. Gather as much information as possible. What does their website look like? How do they get the word out about their practice? How hard do they work? How many years have they been working to build their practice?

Consider everything about that practice, and take notes as you go along. You cannot skip your homework here. Gather the information necessary to see what sets that business apart. Doing this investigative work will help you identify what you need to start doing to reach the same level of success. As in most fields, you don't need to reinvent the wheel. It's already there, and someone is using it successfully. Learn all you can from that person and their business, so that you can begin to emulate their successful qualities.

> *"Formal education will make you a living; self-education will make you a fortune." – Jim Rohn*

Smart students of history investigate those in their field who have come before them. They are serious in their homework. Famous comedy director Judd Apatow, recalled in a recent interview how, as a child, he would watch recordings of Johnny Carson and re-write the monologues word for word, just to see and feel what it was like to write great comedy. Famous Madison Avenue adman David Ogilvy started the same way in direct-response copywriting, taking the most successful ads ever written and painstakingly rewriting them by hand 500 times, just to experience what it meant to be a great copywriter. I'm shocked at the number of clients paying me over $35,000 per year to provide them with marketing advice who have never driven to the local library and pulled the last 5 years of newspaper and local magazine ads to see what has been done successfully in the past. I'm even more amazed at the doctors who fail to take action after I've given them this million-dollar piece of advice.

I'm no different than you are. I used to be in my own prison, too. I was where you are, starting a practice and not knowing exactly what I needed to do to make it successful, or to reach the level that I wanted to be. But we are responsible for the limits that we put on ourselves. These limits keep us chained up, imprisoned, prevented from reaching our goals. Where are your hands tied, right now, in the growth of your practice? Has someone else come before you and found a way to break free from the chains? Why then are you not intently studying this person like your life depends on it?

If I Can Do This, Anyone Can Do This

When I first started my practice, I had zero patients. None. But I didn't let that stop me. I quickly figured out that nothing was going to happen until I took action. I remembered that I pack my own parachute. And I remembered that I needed a road map, so that I could get started on my journey. Taking action and having the right attitude, instead of feeling sorry for myself, I persevered.

Today, I have one of the largest orthodontic practices in the country, and I spend time speaking, teaching, and guiding others, both those just entering the field and those who are veterans of it. But I can tell you that it didn't just "happen" to me. I had to work at it. I took the time to study the history of the profession, and I made a concerted effort to take my practice seriously. I was not going to stand idly by and hope for the best. I took action to prevent pitfalls and to make things happen that I wanted to happen.

The history of the profession demonstrates that there are two types of doctors in this field: those who stand by, waiting for things to happen, and those who become active and make things happen. I'm the latter kind, and my hope is that you are, too!

"Whether you think you can or think you can't – you're right." – Henry Ford

[3]

Take Action to Take Charge of Every Aspect of Your Life

Dan S. Kennedy

ONCE, DRIVING FROM Cincinnati, Ohio, to St. Louis, Missouri, I was listening to a radio call-in show hosted by a lady psychologist. I no longer remember her name or the name of the caller, but I certainly remember the conversation.

The caller, a woman, 40 years old, in her second marriage, spilled out a load of unhappiness and misery. Her husband didn't pay enough attention to her. Her kids were grown and no longer needed her. She was bored.

Finally the host stopped her and said, "You will continue to be unhappy as long as you depend so much on others to make you happy."

I pulled the car off to the side of the road and jotted that down as a fill in the blank formula:

You Will Continue To Be Un-_____

As Long As You Depend On Others

To Make You _____

Then I wrote down a few examples:
- You will continue to be unimportant as long as you depend on others to make you feel important.
- You will continue to be un-prosperous as long as you depend on others to make you prosperous.
- You will continue to be uninspired as long as you depend on others to make you inspired.

The Miracle Formula for Taking Charge of Every Aspect of Your Life

Let me tell you how this Miracle Formula came to me. The very first seminar I ever attended, now more than 35 years ago, where "success concepts" were presented was a real eye-opener for me. The speaker talked about what he called the most unpleasant success principle in the world. Well, who wants to hear about the most unpleasant anything? But I was there, so I listened. He said, repeatedly, "You are exactly where you really want to be."

Now let me tell you where I was. I had driven to the seminar in a 1960 Chevy Impala, and it was not 1960. When it rained, this sad old car leaked from the top and from the bottom. The seats never dried out; they stayed musky damp in the summer, they froze and cracked in the winter. The car's frame was broken clear through, so its rear end was held up with a contraption of bailing wire, wood blocks and a turnbuckle. But there was no shame for this car. I'd paid just $25.00 for it, on payments, and it was all I could afford at the time. And the condition of the car was symbolic of a few other aspects of my life. So when that speaker said: you are exactly where you want to be – hey, I didn't like that very much.

It took me a while to stop arguing and start thinking.

Then I finally wrote down a "formula" from what I thought about, as a result of his statement. I could give it to you on the back of a matchbook – it doesn't require a whole *book* to give you this – but don't let that diminish its importance. It is my non-humble opinion that this painfully arrived at formula has truly profound importance.

Here it is:

CONTROL = RESPONSIBILITY

RESPONSIBILITY = CONTROL

Everybody wants more control. If you take all your personal, career, financial, and other goals, everything you think you want out of life, and boil all that down to a single overriding objective, it is the desire for greater control. Greater control over finances, present and future. Greater control over your time and lifestyle. Greater control over your kids. Etc., Etc.

Ironically, as much as we desire greater control, we are the ones who give it all away. Every time we say...

- It's the location of our business
- It's the season
- It's the economy
- It's the supervisor who has it in for me
- It's the way I was brought up
- It's my partner/co-worker/spouse/etc.
- It's _____

Each and every time we say an "it's the...." We really *do* two things simultaneously: one, we push away a small weight of responsibility, and that temporarily makes us feel better, but, two, we give up an equal-sized amount of control. Whenever we deny responsibility, we give up control. Get rid of a pound of responsibility, lose a pound's worth of control.

The Miracle Formula in Action: Why Does One Person Prosper and Another Suffer?

I happen to know two people very well who are very much alike. They own two almost identical businesses. Their businesses are in neighboring, very similar towns. My observation is that they are equally skilled in the technical and administrative aspects of their business.

One, Peter E., has struggled for about seven years just to stay in business. He has gained very little if any, financial ground during those years. His life is a day-to-day struggle for survival.

The other fellow, Robert L., started six years ago. His business has grown by 10% to as much as 30% each year, every year. He is now getting ready to turn it into a fortune through franchising.

When I talk with Peter E., I hear a lengthy discourse on all the outside influences that negatively affect his business. The economy, taxes, banks that won't give small business a fair shake, competition from huge corporations, and his list goes on and on and on. Every time I talk with Peter, I hear the same list. A broken record playing over and over again.

I acknowledge, by the way, that these factors do exist. I am frustrated by some of them myself. But the issue is not the existence of these factors. The issue is how much control Peter lets them have over his business. Every time Peter recites his list, he shuffles off responsibility for his situation, and that temporarily helps him feel better. But with the responsibility goes the control.

When I talk with Robert, these matters only occasionally come up. Instead, he talks excitedly about the innovative strategies he has discovered and developed to keep his business growing regardless of external influences. He exhibits healthy curiosity and quizzes me about strategies I've seen or discovered recently that might work for him. "How does that client of yours in x-business deal with this y-problem?" – he wants to know. Often, he'll say something like "I really screwed up on this situation. Let me tell you about the base I missed and what I'm doing about it."

Robert accepts all the responsibility for his success or failure, his errors and his achievements, and because he does, he retains control.

ONLY 5% EXHIBIT SELF-RELIANT BEHAVIOR

Years ago, I did a speaking tour of all the CEO Clubs in the country for Joe Mancuso's Center For Entrepreneurial Management, and I talked with groups of corporate presidents in nearly a dozen different cities. If I heard it from one CEO, I heard it from a dozen: "It's getting harder and harder to find worthy people to promote from within."

"Why is that?" I asked.

"Only about 5% of all the people we employ consistently exhibit self-reliant behavior."

"What do you mean by 'self-reliant behavior'?"

One President answered this way: "Well, take the typists here in the office. They know that a proofreader checks their work for errors, so they rely on her rather than bothering to check their own work and consistently present her with typing done right the first time. Then we've got fifty sales reps in the field. Accounting has to constantly chase and nag every one of them to get their paperwork. My Sales Manager told me the other day that we've got one guy who we give wake-up calls to."

Another President said, "We have about 20 people in the Chicago plant. Only three or four consistently get here on time, ready to work. I figure about 5% of all the people we've ever employed, in all the different jobs, accept full responsibility for successful completion of every aspect of their jobs."

The word "typist" dates this a bit, doesn't it? Sorry to say, this entire situation hasn't improved in the years since I first wrote this. It has gotten worse. Sloppiness is epidemic, from the simplest on-the-job tasks, like putting the correct items in the bag handed through the drive-in window if you're a fast food worker, or knowing how to get to a booked destination if a limo driver, to the more critical, like staying awake if you're an air traffic controller, or delivering the right dosage if you're a nurse in a hospital. The #1 reason business owners fire and replace vendors, suppliers, and professionals is this kind of sloppiness. The #1 complaint I hear today from employers about those they weed out is this sloppiness. It is important to understand that all this sloppiness represents irresponsibility, evidence that the person is not to be trusted.

When you think through what these CEOs said, you have a simple answer to a long list of questions...

- How can I move ahead in my career?
- How can I get a better job?
- How can I start my own business?
- How can I have a better relationship?
- How can I maintain a positive outlook?
- How can I make more money?

Most people have unsaid extensions to these kinds of questions:
- How can I move ahead in my career – when others have more education than I do?.....when the boss likes Steve better than me?
- How can I get a better job – when the economy's so bad?
- How can I start my own business – when I haven't got any money?
...and so on.

The answer to these questions and many more like them is: self-reliant behavior.

How Long Will You Wait Before Taking Charge?

The many times that that I followed General Schwartzkopf on a program, I listened as he posed this rhetorical question: if you are put in charge, when you are put in charge, what should you do? TAKE CHARGE!

He was talking about the very essence of leadership – not waiting, not procrastinating, not looking around to copy how others did it or are doing it, not waiting for a committee to cover your butt with its recommendations; instead, stepping forward to do what needs to be done and to do what is right.

All too often, even when an individual finally gets the chance to be "in charge" that he has coveted, he accomplishes little. For years, other players on the NBA Chicago Bulls grumbled and groused about being stuck in the shadow of Michael Jordan. They coveted the chance to command that spotlight and lead the team. But when Michael Jordan retired, that spotlight searched vainly for that team's next leader. In 1994, it couldn't find one. The most logical heir-apparent embarrassed himself and his entire team in the playoffs by throwing a hissy fit over not being named by the coach as the man to get the ball and try the final shot in the final seconds of a closely contested playoff game. This would-be leader let his ego control his actions. Incredibly, he refused to go back in from the time out and give his best efforts to the play that had been called. You can look around and see such individuals squandering their opportunities constantly in just this way.

But I would go even farther: why wait until you are put in charge? Take charge anyway. The fact is: there's a leadership vacuum just about everywhere. Maybe in your home. Probably in your business or place of employment. In your industry, in your community, in your church, in your country. And I suggest this leadership vacuum offers you the opportunity you seek to change your life for the better. Let me give you a very down-to-earth example:

Mary S. was at a seminar I presented for doctors some years ago. She was there with her husband, a dentist. She pulled me aside on a break.

"Could I talk to you alone for a minute?" So she and I ducked out of the meeting room, went down the hall, and found an empty meeting room to step into.

"I'm so frustrated," she told me. "There are so many things you've been talking about that we could do to build up the practice. We keep going to seminars, hearing good ideas, but my husband never gets anything new implemented. Nothing happens. The staff now knows that when he comes back from a seminar talking about new ideas, all they have to do is wait a few days and it'll all blow over. And the practice hasn't grown a bit in three years."

"What kind of things would you have him do?" I asked.

"Join the Chamber of Commerce, attend meetings and make contacts with other business people in the community," she said. "And start a mailing campaign to area business owners and executives. And put out a monthly newsletter for our past and present patients. And put together a little how-to book, something like "How to Keep Healthy Teeth for Life." And, in the office, our reception area desperately needs to be re-decorated. The staff needs some help with handling telephone calls, especially from new patients calling in because of our yellow pages ad. And –"

"Wait a minute," I raised my hand like a traffic cop and brought her to a halt. "Mary, these all sound like inarguably good ideas to me."

"But he won't do any of them," she said sadly.

"Well, Mary," I asked, "What are you waiting for?"

For the first time that night, Mary was speechless. She returned to the meeting room with a particularly thoughtful look on her face.

You see, it's one thing to complain about another person's failure. And it's quite another to pick up the ball and run with it. In this case, Mary was certainly justified in being frustrated with her husband's lack of ambition and initiative. But she'd been complaining to him and about him for three years. She'd been frustrated for three years. Obviously, that wasn't going to change anything. Her only apparent options: accept him and things exactly as-is and stop being aggravated, continue being frustrated every day of her life for the rest of her life, divorce him and leave, or pick up the ball and do some running of her own.

Most would choose one of the first two options. Thoreau observed, "Most men (and women) lead lives of quiet desperation."

About a year later, Mary S. appeared at another of my many seminars for doctors. Again she cornered me on a break, apart from her husband. "I want to tell you," she began, "that I was very angry with you and the way you answered me that night. I wanted some sympathy. And I wanted you to go have a tough talk with my husband. But I sure didn't want you to challenge me."

"Should I apologize?" I asked.

"Hardly," she answered. "Let me tell you about my new life." Mary no longer worked in the office as a dental assistant. Instead she had hired her replacement, then appointed herself Director of Marketing. She joined the Chamber of Commerce, a businesswomen's club, a Toastmasters group, and enrolled in a Dale Carnegie class. She assembled a book – *Secrets of a Healthy Smile for Life* – and she began speaking to groups of school children, PTA meetings, civic groups, everywhere she could on behalf of the practice. She put together a practice newsletter, assigned writing tasks to other staff members and occasionally even to patients, and got it done, published and out every month. She designed a new Family Plan to promote to the practice's patients. She created and promoted Patient Appreciation Weeks.

In five months, the practice doubled. Although shocked at first, her husband adapted to her new role and new interests. And he was kept pretty busy just handling the new patient flow anyway.

"Now I work just three or four hours a day, doing all the marketing and promotion for the practice – I'm our 'Mrs. Outside,' he's our 'Mr. Inside,' and I've even got time for my new venture, creating and publishing health-related coloring books for kids, distributed through dentists nationwide. I'm not waiting anymore," she concluded.

Now, what are you waiting for?

"Are you pleased with your present place in the world? If your answer is yes, what's your next port of call? If your answer is no, what are you going to do about it?" – Earl Nightingale

[4]

Take Action to Manage Every Aspect of Your Success

Dustin S. Burleson

WHEN IT COMES to managing a business, there is one name that stands out above all others – Peter Drucker. Although he died several years ago at the age of 95, he left a legacy on the topic of management that will be difficult for others to surpass. Considered an expert, or guru, on the topic, he brought the idea of management to the forefront – a place where it has remained ever since.

Management is the idea behind taking charge of every aspect of your life. This includes your practice. It would be great if we could open the doors to our practice and just kick back and wait for things to happen. Just wait for the patients to begin calling and coming in for their appointments. But as much as we may want that to happen and as nice as it would be, it's not likely to ever happen. In reality, if you want to be successful, in both your personal and business lives, you have to make things happen. You do that by taking charge, or managing every aspect of your life.

If there is an important lesson that I have learned over the years in practice is that I cannot do it alone. Neither can you. Running a successful dental or orthodontic practice is a team effort. But that team is only going to help you reach your goals if you are a great manager and make the right moves and decisions to begin with. What do I mean by that? Going back to Drucker, in management theory he placed an emphasis on making sure that you lead others and are effective at it. He also believed it was crucial to hire the right people to be on your team.

Hire the wrong people and no matter how good of a coach or manager you are, there is a chance you will never get those people off the bench and into the game. They may never care who wins or pay attention that there is a game going on. They are too busy focusing on a million other things that have nothing to do with your practice or their job. But on the flip side, if you hire the right people, it can do wonders. Hiring the right talent to work in your office can make a tremendous difference in the success of your practice and in how easy it is for you to manage. The right people come together as a team to make your management duties easier. They understand your goals, missions, and philosophy, and they work to help carry them out.

MEASURING, THEN MANAGING

Imagine if you opened the doors of your practice and a year later a colleague asked you how it was going and if you were having success. You scratch your head and say that you really don't know if it is successful. I suppose if the doors are still open there is some level of success present, but that certainly doesn't tell the whole story. Maybe you are biding time having the doors open. Perhaps you are only doing a fraction of what your business is actually capable of doing in your area.

The problem here is that if you don't measure things, you can't really know for sure if your business is successful. Within your practice, it is important to have things to measure. These things will help you determine if you are headed in the right direction, growing as a company, and if you are successful.

So how will you measure success at your practice? Is it the number of repeat patients you have? How about the dollar amount of business you do each year? Or perhaps it is measured in the satisfaction you get out of loving what you do each day. There are many ways to measure, but you have to have something to measure. Only then can you determine if you are reaching goals, as well as the level of success you would like to have in your practice.

"If you can't measure it, you can't manage it." – Peter Drucker

What One Thing = One Answer

I work with private coaching clients on a regular basis. They come to me because they are seeking the wisdom and guidance that it takes to have a successful practice. I've been there, I've created it, and they want the blueprint for doing the same on their own. It's a wonderful thing to be able to help guide others to do what it is that you know they want to do, and that you have done as well. We gain when we teach others, spread the message, and give people the guidance they need in order to reach their goals.

Over and over, I get one question that is always the same. This happens with most people that I work with in private coaching. They all want to know:

"What one thing should I be doing right now?"

My answer is always the same: Everything.

If you focus on doing just one thing, there is a good chance you will not meet your goals and create the practice that you are dreaming of. You have to get really good at doing a lot of things and build a team around you that can help you manage all of the critical components to growing your business. Let me explain.

Anyone who has spent some time with me or that knows me well knows I like to sail. A lot. I talk about it and share stories of my sailing adventures with others. It gives me a lot of pleasure to hit the open waters, absorb the breeze, melt away any stress, and manage the multitude of systems in my boat in order to guide my sail and reach my destination.

When you sail, you have to focus on doing more than one thing, just like in having a successful dental or orthodontic practice. If you were to go out sailing and you only focused on one thing, there is a good chance that you will not only end up somewhere you hadn't intended, but you may drown, or both. Sailing, just like running a successful practice, requires frequent monitoring of many things, including weather conditions, water conditions, sail trim, passengers on board, deckhands, the conditions of the equipment on the boat, and more. There are many things you need to be aware of, monitor, and manage on that sail boat if you want to safely reach your destination. The same can be said for having a successful practice.

Whether you are fit to set sail on a journey requires the knowledge of so many things. There is no way you could set sail with just "one thing" on your mind. So why is it then that doctors wish to run their practices with just one thing, seeking one thing to focus on right now? In all honesty, there are hundreds of little things you must constantly focus on, sometimes intently and sometimes at a distance or through delegation. But one must always have multiple wheels in motion when running any business, and a dental or orthodontic practice is no exception.

"Action is the foundational key to all success." – Pablo Picasso

TAKING THE STEPS

Hearing that you need to manage things and think of everything may seem like a daunting task. You may even feel a bit overwhelmed if you begin to think of all the little things that it takes to run a successful practice. From having someone open the mail and pay the bills to marketing and patient care, there is a wide spectrum of tasks that need to be met. And not just met, but done successfully and effectively. But don't let that scare you and get you heading in the other direction. It's not nearly as complicated and overwhelming as it may seem.

Yes, there is a lot to do. A lot. But that doesn't mean you need to know how to be an expert at doing it all. Not by a long shot. One thing you need to know how to do is manage. Being an effective manager is crucial to a business's success. Like a coach, you need to know who to put in the game, how to get the best out of them, and what each person is capable of doing. You certainly don't need to master all the tasks yourself. You just need to know how to put the right people in each position so that the tasks are carried out for you.

In being a good manager of my practice, I have taken the time to put the right people into key positions. By doing that, I can make sure that even the small tasks are completed and exceeded. Knowing that I have taken care of making sure the smaller tasks are cared for, I can focus on the larger issues.

One problem that many managers have is with delegating. When I say that you need to think of everything, I don't mean that you must be the one to do everything. Not only would it leave you exhausted, but you would be spending less time doing the dental and orthodontic work in your office and more time on a variety of other tasks. Effective managers delegate to people who they know they can trust to carry out the mission.

Surrounding yourself with a team of people who can help you carry the ball and assist you effectively is crucial to your business success. Because of this, don't take the hiring of people lightly. Just like you would be very selective in who you would hire to help you sail a boat around the world, don't throw caution to the wind when it comes to finding superstars to help you run your practice. Always take the time to make sure that the right people are put into each position. That way, everything is taken care of.

> *"If you're trying to achieve, there will be roadblocks. I've had them; everybody has had them. But obstacles don't have to stop you. If you run into a wall, don't turn around and give up. Figure out how to climb it, go through it, or work around it."* – Michael Jordan

READJUSTING AS NEEDED

People are often afraid to take the first steps. They fear that taking action may end up proving to be the wrong action. What if your goal is to build a successful practice and you end up taking action to do A, B, and C, only to find out that you really should have done A, D, and E? That's okay, too!

There is a good chance that, even when you take action and it proves to not be the best course of action, you can use that as a learning experience. Sometimes we have to head in the wrong direction in order to realize that we are going in the wrong direction. In the business world, we cleverly call it "testing the market." McDonald's did it in the 90's when they tested serving made-to-order pizza in their stores. Starbucks did it in the early 2000's when they introduced hot and greasy-smelling breakfast sandwiches that ruined their famous coffee aroma. Both were tremendous failures and both realized it quickly. They redirected their focus and went back to the things that work. The genius in Starbucks and McDonald's wasn't in their willingness to test new ideas. They were both horrible ideas, in hindsight. It's what they did once they realized they were headed in the wrong direction that really counts. It is the same in your business when you realize you are headed in the wrong direction. You have a choice at that point. You can keep going in the wrong direction, knowing you should be going the other way and complaining with every turn. Or you can take action and get headed back in a different direction, to a better route. Don't fear failure, because there is nothing that you are going to do that you can't change if you realize that it can be done better by going in another route.

Peter Drucker once said that "The entrepreneur always searches for change, responds to it, and exploits it as an opportunity." As an entrepreneur who is working at building a successful practice, it is important to realize that you will inevitably change courses and routes along the way. While your main goal of having a successful practice remains constant, you may change your ideals along the way of what it takes to get there and what you want it to include. There is nothing wrong with that. We grow and change as people and it stands to reason that things like our business will do the same.

So long as you take action to get started you can rest assured knowing that you can re-adjust as needed. Your route is not set in stone. It is just something to get you started. The most important thing is that you get started taking action and managing your life. Only then will you find that the things happen that you want to happen. You can change every aspect of your life once you begin to take action. Where you are now in your life is exactly what you want and exactly what you have managed to produce up until now. If you don't like it, what's stopping you from changing it?

"If you don't like where you are in life, change it. You do not have roots. You are not a tree. – Jim Rohn

[5]

Take Action to Get the Know-How You Need

Dan S. Kennedy

NOT KNOWING HOW to do something has never stopped me from setting out to do it, and I've become convinced that anybody can become competent, even expert at just about anything; there are books, courses, classes, teachers, mentors, coaches, newsletters, associations, an absolute abundance of information linked to virtually any and every skill or ability or occupation you can think of. A whole lot of it is readily available, free. More at very modest cost. Some, pricey.

30

The Internet has made it ridiculously easy to obtain information, education, and training. The trek to the library has been replaced by a button, by typing in a search term. Almost every provider of training offers a lot of it free at their web sites as outreach for new customers, just as we do at www.NoBSBooks.com and www.DanKennedy.com, and at www.Pete-The-Printer.com. YouTube is full of video presentations on every imaginable subject by authors, experts, speakers. Any industry and most competitors and many prospective clients or customers can be thoroughly researched without leaving your easy chair, via the Web. Yet, with all this easy access, I find people getting lazier and lazier about doing any homework at all. Professionals who go to some trouble and exert effort to get a meeting with me, to attempt to sell me their services, have not even bothered to Google® me before the appointment. New clients who meet with me often lack even the most basic statistical information about their target market readily, easily available to them at their own trade association's web site. People with problems they seek advice for have not even bothered to investigate what information is available.

Please hear this: absence of intellectual curiosity about both the specific business or other pursuit you are engaged in, about success in general, and even about the world around you produces the same basic result as if you had the I.Q. of a tree frog. Further, failure to act on intellectual curiosity in a constant way is simple evidence of lack of true ambition. I am fond of telling of being backstage with Donald Trump at an event where we were both speakers and, after brief conversation, being asked by The Donald: what three books are you reading now? There's much to be learned by the question. And there's another lesson in the end of the story I usually don't tell because of time. He scribbled down one of the titles I mentioned, handed the paper scrap to an assistant hovering behind him, and said, "Get me this book."

Most people stop far, far, far short of aggressive, ambitious intellectual curiosity – they don't even demonstrate any initiative or self-reliance when it comes to their own work, their own business, and the specific know-how needed for it. I am frequently amazed and dismayed at the people who seek me out and ask questions that evidence they haven't even done an ounce of homework or research on their own. A business owner came to me after I finished delivering a speech on advertising and marketing, handed me the advertising flyer he'd prepared and invested his hard-earned money in having printed and distributed, and said, "What do you think?"

I had a few questions of my own. "Before you put this together," I said, "what books did you go and get about writing advertising headlines? About advertising in general?" And I could have asked a dozen more questions along these same lines. The answers, were, frankly, pitiful. Non-existent. He had done nothing, nada, zero to prepare himself for the task of putting together effective advertising flyers. When you look at this objectively, from the outside in, it's pretty obvious that this is stupid behavior. And quite bluntly, if you insist on behaving stupidly, you do not deserve positive results.

Ignorance about any particular subject is forgivable and, fortunately, fixable. Stupidity is another story altogether.

THE SERIOUS STUDENT AT WORK

When I became earnest about using more humor in my speeches and seminars, and getting good at using it, for example, I found no shortage of assistance out there. Beyond simply observing and analyzing great humorists and comedians, I found plenty of books on the subject, Esar's Comic Encyclopedia, videos, seminars, newsletters, and home study courses. I learned timing from listening to a fantastic humorous speaker, Dr. Charles Jarvis, from comedian Shelley Berman, and others, over and over and over again. I read all the classic masters – Benchley, Thurber, I read all the contemporary humorists, I read everything Steve Allen ever wrote, I found old comedy records, I subscribed to humor services like Orbens. I became a very serious student of humor. Gradually I transitioned from picking and telling jokes to creating original material, from jokes to humorous stories. I did a whole lot of homework. I became accomplished enough at it to make a great deal of money as a professional speaker and, as writer, consultant, and coach, help a lot of other speakers improve their efficacy. I even wrote a book about the use of humor in selling, as speaker or writer: *Make 'Em Laugh And Take Their Money.*

When I got involved in teaching advertising, marketing, and sales to doctors of chiropractic, I became a serious student of the chiropractic profession. I subscribed to the profession's journals, I got and read books, I visited offices, I went to seminars, I asked questions of doctors. In a few months, I knew enough and sounded so much like a chiropractor, that we had to continually correct doctors who called me "Dr. Kennedy" and convinced themselves I was one of them. To this day, I'll be walking through a hotel lobby, airport, or mall and have a chiropractor yell out, "Hello, Dr. Kennedy!" And, although I would never give an adjustment, I can do a decent exam, a good report of findings, I can sell people on chiropractic better than most chiropractors, and I could operate a practice. I could go to a convention and easily pass myself off as a doctor if I chose to. I'll bet I could go to an office and get myself hired as an associate doctor.

Some years back, I worked closely with a client in the retail theft control business. His company dealt with employee and deliveryman theft in supermarkets, convenience stores, and drugstores (where it is an immense problem). Then I subscribed to all the trade journals of the supermarket, convenience store, and drugstore industry, and assembled articles about theft from several years of back issues. I read what books I could find on the subject. I studied my client's materials. I learned the language of retail finance. To this day, I can walk into any such store or restaurant and, in 5 minutes, tell you whether or not the employees are stealing and, if so, show you the "hidden evidence" that proves it. And I could give a seminar to retailers on the subject and no one would question my status as an expert.

I'm not bragging. I'm just pointing out that it isn't very difficult to quickly acquire expertise in a given area, if that's what you want to do. But it's amazing to me the number of people who just never bother.

When I worked with the chiropractors, I used to ask groups for a show of hands – how many had really studied even one book or course on how to sell. In most groups, less than half; yet everyday, their incomes depend on their effectiveness at selling...selling the public and new prospective patients on chiropractic, selling new patients their recommendations and their fees. They're not alone. Just about every business or occupation is a composite of several different types of expertise, but most people master one and are content being an amateur in the others.

If not knowing about something stands between you and what you want to accomplish, get busy and go get that know-how. It really is that simple.

THE 7 WAYS TO GET SMARTER ABOUT VIRTUALLY ANY SUBJECT – FAST

1. Find and read at least a year's back issues of the related trade or specialty magazines.

   Every business, industry, occupation, vocation, hobby or special interest – from cooking to computer programming, from ostrich farming to searching for lost gold mines, from long-haul truck driving to golfing, from writing to woodworking, from Astrology to Zoology – has one, in most cases, several magazines all its own. In these magazines, the experts write articles, are interviewed and profiled, how-to secrets are revealed, advertisers promote their wares.

2. Answer a lot of the ads you find in these magazines.

   Let all those advertisers try to sell you their products and services. Soon, you'll be deluged with information. All coming to you, free.

3. Find the top experts, the most successful people and the most celebrated people in the field.

   Such people have probably written books or recorded audio programs, they may sell such products, seminars, consulting, and coaching, and they may even be approachable just to talk with or visit with free. Seek out the best and the brightest and find out how you can best turn their experience into your knowledge. Surprisingly, even in competitive fields, these outspoken experts and super achievers exist.

Some years back, I worked with a chiropractor who started his own practice immediately after school. Almost immediately. First, armed with a list he had painstakingly compiled of 50 of the most successful, most respected chiropractors in the country, he got in his car and drove across the country, north, south, east and west, going to each of their offices, asking if he could observe, take the doctor to lunch or dinner and pick his brain, visit with the staff, and so on. Forty-nine of the fifty were gracious, generous, encouraging, and helpful. He arrived home with what he called *A Master Practice-Building Plan from the Masters of the Profession.* He had great confidence in this plan. He implemented it with natural enthusiasm and positive expectation. And he built a record-breaking practice in short order.

If I were to start in a brand new business today, I would follow his example.

4. Find the books written by "the OLD masters."
   Just about every field has "old masters", whose works are hard to find or even out of print, who many ignore as passed by time and no longer important. They're wrong.

   In the selling field, every salesperson should read books by Frank Bettger, Red Motley, Robert Trailins, to name a few, from the 1950s, the 1940s, and earlier if you can find them. Robert Trailins' "old book", *Dynamic Selling*, published by Prentice-Hall a long time ago, to be found only in libraries or used bookstores, offers better advice on crafting powerful appointment-getting presentations than any book, seminar or course I'm aware of.

   In direct-response advertising and copywriting, today's top pros, like my friends Gary Halbert and Ted Nicholas, and I, constantly refer novices to the works of the "old masters," Robert Collier, Claude Hopkins, Victor Schwab and others, dating back to the 1930s.

I would add, of course, the suggestion that you read *my* books, and I'm reluctant to say it, but I'm reaching the "old master" status. For selling, read my *No B.S. Sales Success* book. For marketing, read *No B.S. Direct Marketing for Non-Direct Marketing Businesses*, as well as *The Ultimate Marketing Plan* and *The Ultimate Sales Letter*. For entrepreneurship, read *No B.S. Business Success* and *No B.S. Wealth Attraction for Entrepreneurs*. They're all readily available at bookstores, BN.com, and amazon.com, or you can get free information about them at www.NoBSBooks.com.

5. Join trade associations or clubs.

The learning curve shortcuts available through trade association membership and attending association conventions and workshops is remarkable. The opportunity to make dozens and dozens of important and beneficial contacts is even greater.

Most associations have archives of audio recordings from past years' conventions and workshops, so you can "attend" two, five, even ten years of past events as if a time machine were at your disposal.

Many national associations have state, regional or city chapters, with easily accessible meetings and seminars, usually all at very modest costs.

At Glazer-Kennedy Insider's Circle™, we now have local chapters and coaching groups, and you can find information about them at dankennedy.com. If you received this book from a business expert in a particular field, he may offer options for coaching and mastermind groups to join as well.

WHY DO TOP PERFORMERS USE COACHES?

When the legendary golfer Arnold Palmer needed to tune-up his game, to compensate for his age, he sought out a young-by-comparison, 26 year old swing coach. This should not surprise. It's widely known that virtually all top athletes in every sport rely on coaches. But why do top sales professionals, small business owners, professionals in private practice, entrepreneurs, authors, speakers, and executives need coaches too?

Having personally had over 400 high-flying entrepreneurs and self-employed professionals in my own coaching programs, having assisted with coaching programs and groups reaching thousands in fields like chiropractic, dentistry, and financial services, and having been a leader and innovator in the development of business coaching, thus essentially spawning hundreds of niche-industry coaches, in aggregate coaching nearly one million people, I think I have a pretty good understanding of why coaching seems to work so well for so many top performers in business. There are six reasons:

1. Being Questioned and Challenged
2. Being Held Accountable
3. Being Listened To
4. Being Accepted
5. Being Motivated
6. Being Recognized For Achievements

Different people have different needs at different times in their lives and different stages of development in their businesses, but everyone can benefit from some at any and every time.

QUESTIONED AND CHALLENGED

The more successful you are, the less likely the people who work for you or are around you all the time are going to challenge your ideas. It's easy to wind up surrounded by "yes men" – and to like it! The outside coach with no axe to grind can be both objective and frank. Most importantly, he can ask the provocative questions that force you to defend and, at times, re-evaluate your ideas.

HELD ACCOUNTABLE

On many occasions, as a speaker, I have been backstage in "green room" conversations with legendary athletes like NFL quarterbacks Joe Montana and Troy Aikman, Olympian Mary Lou Retton, boxer-turned-super entrepreneur George Foreman, coaches like Tom Landry, Jimmy Johnson, Lou Holtz. The athletes all agreed that top performers personally hold themselves accountable to gruelingly high standards, but still, were it not for accountability to teammates, fans, and coaches, and being held accountable by coaches who monitor their statistics, show them film and critique it, and work with them for improvement, they would never have reached the levels of success they did. Every coach agrees that the very act of reporting to someone and being held accountable by someone automatically improves performance. A business/life coach can ably fulfill this need.

LISTENED TO

A *Newsweek* article about professional business and life coaches described us as "part therapist – part consultant." That's fair. A lot of entrepreneurs, executives, and sales pros have no one to talk to about business or personal matters who they can dare "let their hair down" with....who will listen without agenda of self-interest or judgment...who can serve as a sounding board. I find, often, that a client will talk his way to his own terrific answer, solution, or plan of action if I'll just listen. Having to discuss your business, goals, problems, ideas, and questions with a knowledgeable coach who listens forces you to stop, think, focus, and organize your own thoughts and sometimes acquire or assemble information – all valuable action that otherwise may take a perpetual back-seat to day-to-day activity. A great coaching question originally posed by author Joe Karbo is: "Are you too busy making a living to make any real money?" A coach can forcibly slow you down, get you off the hamster wheel you're running on, and insist that you think through your intentions and actions out loud. In group coaching environments, the famous strategist Jay

Abraham and I call this "hot-seating"; putting you on the hot seat, in front of the group, thinking out loud and being aided or questioned as you go, everybody working without a net.

ACCEPTED

I call myself and my most successful clients "Renegade Millionaires" – but we are seen by most around us as misfits, loose cannons, difficult and unreasonable people, and aggravations! Because we Renegade Millionaires violate most industry norms, reject traditions and limits, aggressively and determinedly push forward our ideas, and because, candidly, we are both exceptionally effective and surprisingly dysfunctional in one way or another, we think, talk, and act very differently from almost everyone around us in daily life. A lot of successful entrepreneurs suffer isolation and loneliness, feel like "fish out of water", even have trouble explaining themselves and what they do to "civilians". Being part of a mastermind group comprised of like-minded renegades, organized, facilitated, and coached by a capable leader, is invigorating. One of the core human needs is to be accepted for who you are, without need of mask or cautious editing of expressed thought, and a relationship with the right coach provides that.

MOTIVATED

Surely a top pro athlete paid millions of dollars to play a game doesn't need to be "motivated," right? Actually, the fact that they are paid millions of dollars, win, lose or draw, means they do need a great deal of other motivation. In almost every locker room, grown men paid millions are awarded game balls and trophies. Coaches cry, hug, atta-boy! Ultimately, all motivation is self-motivation, but it is fueled by the people and ideas you associate with, the successes of others you're exposed to, the encouragement you get. Paul J. Meyer, one of "the grand old men" of the success philosophy field and founder of Success Motivation Institute gave a speech entitled "Who Motivates The Motivator?", pointing out that leaders must accept personal responsibility for their own motivation, but that everybody needs motivational influencing.

Recognized For Achievements

Everybody thrives on recognition and celebration – but to whom can the entrepreneur brag? Certainly not his employees, competitors, or vendors. It's hard for an entrepreneur to be welcomed home as a conquering hero. A good coach, singly or in concert with a mastermind group, who understands and genuinely appreciates your accomplishments, fills an important gap in entrepreneurial life.

What Exactly Is Business / Life Coaching?

Coaching is delivered in many different ways: one-to-one, in person, by phone or online; one-to-group, in mastermind meetings and workshops and field trips; via tele-seminars, webinars, and peer-to-peer online resources; and combinations and hybrids thereof. It sometimes has prerequisite study of certain courses or resources, attendance at certain seminars, or the meeting of certain income or other qualifications. It is priced by the hour or day, by the month, by the year, or through a fee for a program. Sometimes, coaching programs also include support services and/or done-for-them tools and resources to use in your business. Some coaching programs or groups are strictly limited in size, while others are open; some feature territorial exclusivity or competitor lock-out, most do not. Ethical coaches do two primary things: one, structure their relationship with and deliverables for clients to be as valuable and effective as possible for those who implement them, and two, exert best efforts to select clients they genuinely believe will benefit and profit from their coaching. It has to be said that buying coaching is not a substitute for implementation!

Take Action to Expand Your Business Skill Set

DUSTIN S. BURLESON

WHEN YOU THINK of some of the best athletes in the world, there are a couple of names that inevitably come to mind. Michael Jordan and Tiger Woods for starters. And when you think of those two people who are top athletes in each of their respective fields, you see a superstar. You see someone who makes a lot of baskets and sinks a lot of golf balls. But what you don't see are the coaches behind them who have worked to help those athletes hone their skills and bring out their best.

That's right, even people like Michael Jordan and Tiger Woods have, or have had, coaches. Even all the talent in the world doesn't mean that you know how to put it to use or that you can't do something better. Michael Jordan is certainly a talented basketball player. But he always had coaches who saw different things in him and were able to help him unlock that potential and talent and bring out his best. Some people may feel intimidated when it comes to challenging such great athletes, but a coach doesn't. A coach has what it takes to challenge them, which will help them to grow as people and professionals.

In his book entitled *How I Play Golf*, Tiger Woods writes about how his coach, Butch Harmon, taught him a valuable skill. During the 1995 U.S. Amateur at Newport Country Club, his coach taught him how to have a successful shot in windy conditions. He had the skills needed to see it through, but first he needed to learn it. He goes on to say that it is a shot that he has used many times during windy conditions because it is so effective.

Coaches can sometimes help you see new angles, new directions, or help you open your eyes to see what is right in front of you the whole time. It's kind of like the old saying, that at times we can't see the forest for the trees. The same holds true in your practice. You, like so many others, get stuck doing the same thing over and over and you don't see what you could, or should, be doing. Getting an outside opinion from a coach can be one of the best moves you ever make. That goes for those who are world-class athletes as well those who want to have a successful dental or orthodontic practice.

> *"I've missed more than 9000 shots in my career. I've lost almost 300 games. 26 times, I've been trusted to take the game winning shot and missed. I've failed over and over and over again in my life. And that is why I succeed." –* Michael Jordan

Taking Action

Without a doubt, there are going to be things in your practice that you do not know how to do, or how you could be doing those things better. But you are faced with a choice when this happens. You can either keep doing things the same way, over and over again, or you can look for something better. That something better may not be easy for you to identify, but usually a coach is a good answer.

Coaches evaluate, assess, guide, challenge, review, and help you get results. Working with them is an invaluable tool. Where would Michael Jordan and Tiger Woods be had they never taken their interests and talents and developed them further by working with coaches?

Just think of where you may never be if you don't further develop your skills and knowledge. Whether you do it by reading more books, attending workshops, or working with a coach, there is a lot to be gained, no matter what field one is in.

Each month, there are one billion unique users that visit YouTube. Combined, they watch over four billion hours worth of videos each month. That's a lot of video watching! Sure, Psy and Justin Bieber may take the top spots for the most views. But there is something else going on here as well. YouTube has become a place where people can go to learn about anything and everything. Want to see how an eye cornea transplant is done? How about how to fix your toilet? There are videos on these two topics and so much more, all on YouTube. People can learn about whatever it is that they want, and need, to learn about, and they can do it through a variety of methods. Gone are the days when you had to head to the library to learn how to do things or how things were done. It's all at the touch of a finger on the computer.

This brings me to my next point, which is something that was discussed in the prior chapter. It's taking the time to learn what it is that you need to learn. I have personally invested hundreds and hundreds of thousands of dollars in coaching and consulting. I am constantly tinkering, like a cat with a ball of yarn, to untangle the next clue, the next breakthrough, the next discovery in my journey to a more successful practice.

I can say that without a doubt all the coaching and consulting has paid off. Today I have a successful practice and I'm where I want to be, although there is always room for growing and improving. As we discussed in the first chapter, there are those who are constantly questioning coaching and consulting and just seeing them as expenses, and then there are those who see the costs as an investment. One that is going to pay off a considerable return. The difference in these two types of people? Those who take massive action on their coaching and consulting knowledge will see massive results and return on investment.

"An investment in knowledge pays the best interest." – Benjamin Franklin

INVESTING IN YOURSELF

When you think about what you spent to become the doctor that you are, it is clear that you have invested a great deal. Not just in money, but you have also invested a great deal of time. You have spent years hitting the books, sitting through lectures, taking exams, and performing procedures. So much has already been invested. But to get to where you want, like most doctors you will need to invest a little more.

Investing additional time by working with a coach, reading books, attending workshops, and doing a variety of other things will help to round out and build upon what you already have. You have all the skills and education that it takes to successfully perform dental and orthodontic procedures, but that doesn't mean you are familiar with how to sell your practice, marketing, hiring the right people to work in your office, and how to determine what needs changing in order to grow your business. That makes sense, after all, because it is not covered in all the things you have focused on during your years of studying to become a doctor in the field.

This is the same idea Dan Kennedy was pointing out with the chiropractors he has worked with. Chiropractors come out of their schooling ready to take on the world and offer all the evaluations and treatments they have been taught. But most have not been given much training in the area of setting up an office, marketing the business, setting goals, growing the business, and determining the best route to take to do each. I think it is safe to say that most dentists and orthodontists experience the same type of thing. You have had the training you need in order to do exams, evaluations, and determine treatments, but you probably haven't had much training or education on how to grow a successful practice. Without that information and guidance, you are missing a big piece of the puzzle.

The good news is that you don't have to spend as much as you did learning your trade in order to gain the necessary skills. You also don't need to put in the same amount of time. Just making the commitment to put in some time will help set you on the right path and get your practice on the right path.

So how do you go about getting the knowledge that you need? Well, you have taken the first step in that direction by reading this book. Now you can take it further by reading more, attending seminars and workshops, and working with a coach who is successful in the field.

"If you want to be successful, find someone who has achieved the results you want and copy what they do, and you'll achieve the same results."
– Tony Robbins

GETTING STARTED

Knowing that something is lacking is the first sign that something needs to change. Doing a self-evaluation and finding that there are things that you may need to gain more knowledge about may be something people shy away from. It may be scary, difficult, or you may dread it because of the time that it will require for you to gain that knowledge. But ask yourself this – what happens if you do nothing? What happens if you don't take the necessary steps to gain that additional knowledge so you can get your practice going in the right direction?

That's right. Nothing happens.

In order for something to happen, for something to change, you have to set the wheels in motion. Reading this book was the first step in admitting there is something more you need. But don't stop there. Set yourself on a course of action, so that you achieve and succeed.

[7]

Take Action to Get Paid

DAN S. KENNEDY

ONE OF THE most interesting metaphysical authors, Stuart Wilde, says "When they show up, bill 'em." What does that mean? It actually refers as much to overriding attitude as to business policy.

One meaning is to properly value your time. If you do not place a high value on your time, I can promise you no one else will. Yet, the one thing we all have an equal amount of is time. Everybody starts out each day with 24 hours to invest as wisely as possible, for profit, for joy, for the benefit of others. The richest man in the world gets not a minute more to work with than does the poorest beggar on the street. But you can bet everything you've got that he thinks about that time differently, feels about that time differently, allocates that time differently, and has an entirely different intellectual, emotional, physical and actual experience with time than does the beggar. There's the rub; to get from poor to rich, you have to adopt the attitudes about time of the rich.

Another meaning, a bigger one, is to value yourself.

When I first started in the success education business, one of the few people in the country who was consistently effective at selling self-improvement audio programs direct, face to face, to executives and salespeople gave me what turned out to be very, very good advice – he said: "Don't waste your time trying to sell these materials to the people who need it most. They won't buy it. You should focus on selling to successful people who want to get even better." Over the years, I've demonstrated the validity of this to myself a number of different ways. And I've developed an explanation for it. There is what I now call "the self-esteem Catch-22 loop" at work here: in order for a person to invest directly in himself, which is what buying self-improvement materials is, he has to place value on himself, i.e. have high self-esteem, but if he has such high self-esteem, he is probably already doing well and does not have a critical need for this type of information; he will get marginal improvement out of it; but the person who needs it most does not place much value on himself, i.e. has relatively low self-esteem, which prohibits him from buying, believing in or using self-improvement materials.

At a very practical level, I see this "value hang-up" surface all the time with entrepreneurs, authors, speakers, consultants, and doctors dealing with fees and prices. I understand it. I still remember the first time I quoted a client $15,000 to develop a direct-mail campaign for him, held my breath, and instantly thought to myself "Geez, Kennedy, a lot of people work all year to make that much money. What business do *you* have asking for that for a few days' work? Who do you think you are anyway?" But here's the amazing thing: the world largely accepts *your* appraisal of your value, and just about everybody under-values and under-prices their contributions.

My good friend Rodney Tolleson was very active for a handful of years in the practice management business, providing doctors of chiropractic with a comprehensive collection of business-building services, training, and counseling. I worked with him doing many of the seminars. We both discovered that these "professionals" were no different than anyone else; they had incredible mental and emotional blocks about charging what they and their service were worth. Although his company provided them with enormously helpful technical, management, and marketing assistance and tools, the greatest income leaps were achieved by focusing on the doctors' beliefs about worth and value – "practice esteem" and "self esteem." There was more "fee resistance" in the doctors' minds than in the public's. And all their actions relative to promoting the practice, stimulating referrals, setting, asking for, and promptly collecting fees, insisting on compliance with recommendations were governed – hindered – by their surprisingly low self-appraisals.

A 'NO B.S. MARKETING LETTER' SUBSCRIBER & INSIDER'S CIRCLE™ MEMBER HITS THE NAIL ON THE HEAD

I'm fortunate to have tens of thousands of Insider's Circle™ Members and Subscribers who are bright, curious, innovative, and contributive, so ours is more of a continuing dialogue than just my publishing a newsletter. One such Member is David Garfinkel, the President of a consulting firm named Let Your Clients Do Your Selling. When I got into the final stages of this book, I invited my Members to submit their ideas about "the ultimate secret of success." David's suggestion was most interesting. And, while it does not name "the ultimate secret," it does hit the nail on the head about the chief obstacle to benefiting from that secret.

David said, "After all the smoke clears, it gets down to one thing – one limiting belief – one self-concept that, once revamped, will set you off on a permanent success trajectory. I think that's different for each of us, but it's usually a personal version of the feeling 'Yes, I really *can* succeed.'"

I agree. For more than 15 years, I have explained that we live inside two boxes:

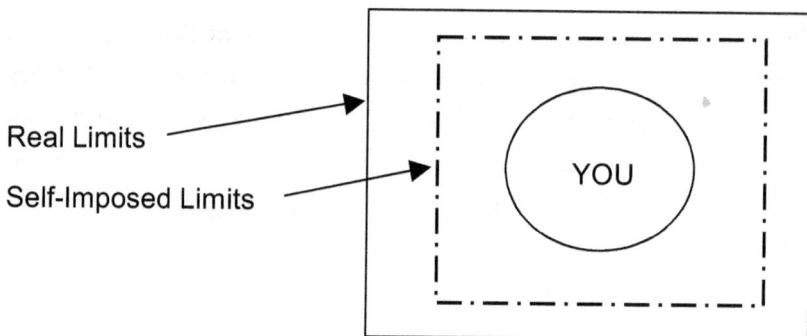

Real Limits

Self-Imposed Limits

YOU

The solid, outer boundary represents *real limits*, and we all have some real limits. For a time, the oldest active player in the NFL was Vince Evans, a back-up quarterback for the Oakland Raiders – playing capably at age 39, the age I was when I wrote this book. More recently, Brett Favre came within a couple of plays of putting the Minnesota Vikings in the Super Bowl as the oldest starting quarterback in the NFL. Still, I really *can't* go try out and make the roster of an NFL team unless I buy one, like the Warren Beatty character in the movie *Heaven Can Wait*. Even if I diligently trained non-stop for the next 12 months, I still couldn't do it. I didn't play in high school or college (I didn't go to college), I'm not big on exercise, I have a bad back made worse by serious injuries while driving in harness races, a bad knee, horrible eyesight. There is a *real* limit making my playing quarterback in the NFL impractical.

As of now, you can't do business on Mars. That's a *real* limit. (Although there is an enterprising fellow who has sold thousands of deeds to imaginatively named lots of land on Mars at, as I recall, $1,000.00 each, by mail-order. Also outer-space related, the bombastic promoter Richard

Branson has collected fee deposits from a lot of people for their flights on his to-be-built, who-knows-when rocket ships.)

There are *real limits* on what you may want to do.

But way inside that solid line, real boundary, is the dotted line. The dotted line represents the *self-imposed limits*. This is a much smaller box we build around ourselves. It's made up of "If", "Can't, "Impossible" inaccurately applied, of negatives in "The Big 4 Of Life": Self-Esteem, Self-Image, Self-Confidence and Self-Discipline. But David's suggestion adds a new wrinkle to all this; that there is *one* dot on this dotted line that is bolder, blacker, bigger and more significant than all the others...and that when you bust through it, the entire dotted line box disappears.

In monetary terms, that dotted line certainly controls how much value you place on yourself, your time, your know-how and your services, how much you dare demand, and how much you get. Anytime you push that box out, you automatically increase your income. I would suggest that the biggest leap can come from pushing against it at the point where it seems strongest.

"Abundance" Doesn't Care

Liberals constantly try to demonize exceptional ambition and achievement. This follows a liberal theme that the economy is and must be "win-lose"; if one person gets "too rich," that must somehow force others to become poor or poorer. This kind of class divisiveness may be necessary politics for the liberals, but it is economic nonsense. And, unfortunately, this is one of the ways people build up guilt about striving for and achieving extraordinary successes.

Foster Hibbard often talked about two men going down to the ocean, one with a teaspoon, the other with a bucket, each taking away the amount of water he chooses to take away. The ocean, however, doesn't care. The ocean doesn't care if you come down there with a teaspoon, bucket, or tanker truck. The ocean is a miraculously replenishing, unlimited resource. That represents *abundance*. And Abundance doesn't care either. It matters not to Abundance whether you tap into it a little or a lot. Your withdrawals don't diminish anyone else's opportunities, nor do they damage the total amount of available abundance. It is infinite. Infinite! And the only limits on your share are placed on you by you.

"What you are willing to accept is what you get." – Dan Kennedy

[8]

Take Action to Discover New Capabilities

Dustin S. Burleson

EVERY ONE OF us is a product of all that we have encountered throughout the years. Not one of us has gotten by without having a vast number of things influence us and the very nature of who we are. The influence can be good or bad, positive or negative. The good influences in our lives tend to often be overshadowed by the less-than-good ones. The negative influences, which tend to stand out in our mind more often than the positive ones, become baggage that we carry around.

This goes for every doctor, too. Every doctor has baggage from his or her upbringing, from the time spent in school, during residency, and more. When you think of all the things that can create baggage in your life, it can seem a bit overwhelming. There is baggage from your spouse, your secular religion that influences how your business operates and how the world operates, and even from actual religion. There are influences everywhere pulling at you all the time.

Some are pulling this direction, while the others are pulling in the complete opposite. Having all of this baggage can cloud your ideals and attitude. It can make you lose focus on what it is that you want and what you need to do to get there. All the baggage impacts your attitude, and if there is one thing that has a major influence over your success in life, it is that of your attitude. The wrong attitude will hold you back, fill you up with excuses, and make you bitter. The right attitude will help you achieve everything you set out to accomplish, and more.

> *"Your attitude, not your aptitude, will determine your altitude."*
> *– Zig Ziglar*

SETTING DOWN THE BAGS

Ever notice when you go to the airport, at least prior to bags having rollers, that you would carry your bags around looking for opportunities to set them down? That's because all the baggage gets heavy. And when you carry it around it tends to weigh on you in other areas. Your muscles may get tired, but so does your mind. You can't concentrate as much because you are concerned with how the strap is digging into your shoulder, or how it is making you feel tired. You just want a break from carrying around all those bags.

It is the same concept in other areas of your life. When you are carrying around all that baggage, no matter where it came from, it weighs on you. The baggage from your upbringing and other areas of your life may consume your mind. It may make it more difficult to concentrate on your goals. Instead, you are too busy worrying about how this or that is bothering you, hurting you, distracting you.

The answer to this is to shed the baggage. In fact, your practice requires you do this if you want to take it to a new level. You will need to purposely shed the baggage and reinstall new ways of thinking about your world, your business, your employees, and your patients. Nothing short of business reinvention is the goal here. It may seem like a daunting task at first, but once you finally set the baggage down and move on, you will feel lighter, think more clearly, and will be able to accomplish so much more.

Just imagine how your life will change if you make the decision that all that baggage is no longer going to weigh you down. It is not going to slow you up, steal your attention, or get in the way of the decisions you make from here on out. Sounds great, right? Believe it or not, you do hold the key to making this a reality. It is all a matter of deciding that those things will no longer control your life and that you want more. Set the bags down, as difficult as it may seem to do so, and walk away. You will be so happy and relieved once you do!

> *"Things may come to those who wait, but only the things left by those who hustle." – Abraham Lincoln*

WHY CARRY THEM AROUND?

Let's say that you packed those bags that were mentioned earlier, the ones that you wanted set down in the airport. Suppose you took the trip, wherever the destination and purpose, and that you made it back home safe and sound. Great! What do you do with the baggage? Do you continue to drag it around with you for the next few weeks, months, or even years? Not unless you are a glutton for punishment!

No, you set the bags down, you walk away. You come back a little later and you put the things in their place. Clothing into hampers and drawers, toiletries into the bathroom. You unpack, ridding yourself of that baggage. The same concept can be used in your everyday life. Things happen to us, and have happened to us throughout our lives. But we should not carry the baggage around, making it harder for us to enjoy life and achieve our goals. No, we set the bags down, we keep going, and we achieve.

That doesn't mean that you can never think about those bags again, or that you deny you ever carried them. But it does mean that you make a conscious decision that you are not going to continue to carry them and let them hold you back anymore.

WORKING SMARTER, NOT HARDER

Doctors are often guilty of thinking that they need to work harder and harder in order to achieve the level of success they dream of or want. They will put in more hours, miss out on family time, and keep grinding away in the office. The thought is that if they could just work harder, they will make it. But that is simply not always the case. Sure, you need a strong work ethic, but that doesn't mean you clock 14 hours per day. It means that you work smarter, rather than harder, in order to achieve those goals.

My father grew up in West Virginia, and the way he grew up may surprise some people. He didn't have running water until he was in the third grade. His mother, my grandmother, cooked over an open fire. No fast food restaurants and dining out every other night for them. When they had to go to the restroom, they had to bundle up in boots and a coat and hike out back to the outhouse.

I know what you are thinking – wow, what an awful way to live. You think this because we have grown accustomed to, and expect, modern day conveniences. Some of these conveniences may have made our life easier, some more so than others, but they haven't been able to replace the life lessons that were gained by living the way my father did when he was growing up.

The upbringing that my father had instilled an incredible work ethic in him, and it was also passed onto me. There are many times when I think the solution is to simply work harder. But then I am reminded that smart doctors, and I like to consider myself in that group, discover that by working smarter they can achieve a tremendous amount. And they can still be home in time to enjoy dinner with their families.

"Believe you can and you're halfway there." – Theodore Roosevelt

TAKING INVENTORY

Now is the time to begin thinking about the baggage you have been carrying around. No matter what it is, consider how it may be holding you back. It may seem difficult to think about setting it down at first, but once you do and you feel the relief it brings, you will be happy you did. Also, evaluate your work ethic and what you think makes for a strong one. Is it putting in as many hours per day as you can, or working smarter? With a little self-assessment you can take action to address these issues and move closer toward your goal of having the practice of your dreams.

Why Even Smart, Talented, Skilled People Fail to Get What They Want from Their Lives

Dan S. Kennedy

IF A FIRE erupts in a crowded theater, most everybody will leap up and hurry from their seats in a mad stampede toward the exits. But how many people, on arrival, take notice of the location of the exits and choose their seats to allow best access to them if needed?

When a need or desire occurs – a leaky roof worsening with each rain or a new car or home to buy – everybody digs into their finances to figure out how they might assemble the money or credit required for that purchase. How many people, do you suppose, have a complex portfolio of pre-determined goals, know the financial requirements of those goals, and benchmark and track their income, savings, and wealth progress day by day or week by week, month by month, year by year?

Most business owners report to work at their place of business quite reliably. But how many arrive with a detailed agenda for the day, including key objectives, pre-set start and stop times for meetings, phone calls and tasks, and a sense of urgency about successfully completing that agenda? Most business owners also advertise, market and promote, but how many do so by a marketing plan and calendar devised for the entire year ahead?...employing systematic outreach for new customers, follow-up on unconverted leads or visitors who don't purchase, follow-up with customers?

(Since training, consulting, and coaching on marketing strategies and systems has been my primary role for over 30 years, I can tell you with authority that the overwhelming majority of business owners as well as salespeople live and die by random acts of sales and marketing, have more holes in the bottom of their buckets than buckets, and can't diagram their step-by-step system for maximum monetization of every lead, every customer, every opportunity in their business, even if you offer them a million dollars for the drawing. They permit randomness in every nook and cranny, from the way their phones are answered to what happens after an appointment with no sale to – everything.)

Almost everybody exerts effort. And in that sense, almost everybody takes action. Yet, the population in general and every sub-population within it organizes itself into a pyramid, with – consistently – 1% at its peak, another 4% near its top, 15% doing well, then a precipitous drop to a big hunk of about 50% that I call The Mediocre Majority, then 30% barely in the game at all. This tells us that action or activity alone has little connection to success and failure. There are many different kinds of action, activity, and effort. For example, in the above paragraphs I wrote of "organized effort." Top professional athletes have carefully organized diet and exercise regimens connected to very specific objectives. Most regular guys show up at the gym and take whatever machine's available. Eat randomly, depending on what's in the 'fridge, cooked, and put on the dinner table in front of them, or where their buddies decide to go for lunch. Everybody has worked out and everybody has eaten, but in the pyramid of fitness, there are 1% in amazing condition, 4% in damned good condition, 15% within the range of good condition, then a precipitous drop. So it is with income, with sales or entrepreneurial or other for-profit personal performance, with companies, with wealth. With any kind of success you want to examine.

Activity asks only one question: are you working? Productivity asks many more complicated and, well, productive questions, in order to break the Work-Money Link. Are you working in the environment most conducive to your success? On the right priorities? In ways that utilize your strengths? On your agenda – or others? With measurement and accountability? And on and on and on. Woody Allen famously said that just showing up accounted for 33% of all success. But it's that other 66% that gets complicated. And it is the willingness to manage self and business with a complicated structure and system for success that differentiates the 1% from the 4%; combined, the 5% from the next 15%; and combined again, the 20% from the 80%.

"ARE YOU TELLING ME, FINGERSTEIN, THAT THERE'S A DIFFERENCE BETWEEN ACTIVITY AND ACCOMPLISHMENT? DAMMIT, WHY WASN'T I INFORMED OF THIS SOONER?"

Copyright © Dan Kennedy 2007   Vincent Palko www.AdToons.com

One of the things to decide, going forward, is how demanding you are going to be of yourself as well as of everyone around you. I have written entire books about these two subjects, which I urge getting and reading: *No B.S. Time Management for Entrepreneurs* and *No B.S. Ruthless Management of People and Profits*. These books are confrontational, and will challenge you.

After I spoke for several hours at a seminar about the subjects of productivity, self-management, accomplishment, and autonomy, a woman approached me, frowning. She said that, while she agreed with everything I said in principle, and certainly wanted the kind of autonomy and success and wealth I'd described, surely there had to be a way to have it all without sacrificing her spontaneity and being so regimented in managing herself and her affairs. She didn't like the rigidity of my approach. I told her that when I flew home that evening by private jet, I had a specific destination at which I intended to arrive safely, without incident, on time, and I hoped my pilots weren't committed to spontaneity. As a shareholder in a portfolio of companies, I chose none based on them having CEO's committed to spontaneity. I'm reasonably confident that Trump often feels like wearing khaki slacks, no socks, and a T-shirt, but he is never seen in public wearing anything but the specific business uniform he has found effective and made a trademark. He is not at all spontaneous about wardrobe, just throwing on whatever he's in the mood to wear. I made no less than a million dollars a year as a speaker for many years, performing a carefully scripted, tested, timed sales speech with such precision you could set your watch by the word. I did not go out there and spontaneously talk about whatever was on my mind any particular day. I make no less than a million dollars a year as a direct-response copywriter and as an influential writer with six newsletters, writing by pre-determined formulas and checklists and disciplines, not by spontaneously writing if, when inspired, on whatever topic captures my interest.

Sorry, kiddo, but everything in the success-store does have a price tag attached, written in ink, non-negotiable.

There are lots of ways to defend failure behavior. Spontaneity is one of many. Characterizing yourself as "an idea person" who just "isn't good at" organization, discipline, and implementation is another. There are even personality assessment tests you can take that will validate such a precept, so you have independent verification of your deficiency. But try depositing that in the bank, or buying your dream home, or funding your retirement with it. You can't walk up to the cash register in the success-store with any of that as accepted currency.

Ultimately, there are only two choices to be made. To continue and endlessly, creatively defend failure behavior...or determine what success behavior is and re-train yourself to practice it – and even to like it.

I used to love everything about drinking and drinking to excess. I used to love a diet of Mexican food, pizza, pasta, and bread, and my favorite breakfast food was doughnuts. I was guilty of swinging into Dunkin Donuts to get two or three to eat in the car en-route to the airport, then having another with coffee at the airport. And I shared President Bush #1's attitude about broccoli. I have re-trained myself to eat a markedly different diet and to avoid alcohol altogether. As I was writing the revisions for this book, I found need to make it even more strict, and I can't honestly say I prefer my new diet versus the old one, nor that I love its rigid restrictions, but I recognize it is the non-negotiable price written in ink for not being fat and woefully unhealthy, for being fit enough to engage in a physically demanding sport as a professional, for managing diabetes without side effect laden drugs and injections – for success. I am 45 pounds lighter than at my worst weight, I've shed it, I've kept it off for years now, only by keeping it off every day, every meal, every snack.

You can retrain yourself for any sufficiently motivational purpose. Whatever the source you wish to credit, humans have capacity for re-invention denied all other living creatures. But not if you cling to old defenses for existent, failure behavior. You can accomplish just about anything you might set out to do, but not without sacrifice of other things. Sorry, but everything in the success-store has a price tag attached, written in ink, non-negotiable. Every road to success has a toll booth and a non-negotiable toll.

Ultimately, forward progress is pretty darned simple. It is about getting productive and profitable things done, as quickly as can be (without sloppy haste that causes undue waste or dangerous recklessness), as consistently as can be. Speed matters. Constancy matters. *Done* matters a lot. Until *doing* becomes *done*, accomplishment is merely an intent and a hope; there is only activity.

If you watch most people, you will realize they are reacting, not proactively determining. They are going through every day like the little metal ball inside an old-fashioned pinball game machine, bouncing and spinning about as the different paddles flip up and hit them. At the end of each such day they are exhausted, and no wonder. At the end of each period of evaluation, month, year, they are disappointed. Random response to external stimuli rarely produces real accomplishment, and to whatever degree it does, it occurs with low efficiency. The flippers in the game can be anything from compulsively checking and indiscriminately responding to e-mails and texts to dealing with whatever customer appears rather than prospecting or marketing to bring the best customers in by appointment. The list of every flipper that people let bounce them about would be as long as this book. It's up to you to identify all in your life and get control of them. That raises its own questions – notably will you? and then, when? There is only one correct answer to that second question, and it is the secret of this entire book.

[10]

Take Action to Make More Money

Dustin S. Burleson

IF YOU ARE like most other doctors, there is a good chance that you have a distorted view of money and your value in the world. Don't worry, it's not your fault, and the good news is that it is something you can change. This is something that happens because we are taught that doctors don't sell things. But if you have the gift to change lives and help people, why would you want to withhold that from anyone? And why wouldn't you want to benefit from it in return?

You want everyone to enjoy the benefits of what it is that you do. But in order for that to happen, you have to change your view regarding money and your value in this world. You help to make the world a better place, without a doubt. If you have doubts about that, just ask a few of your patients who have completed treatment successfully and hear about what it has done for them. Listen to their stories as they share how it has helped to make them happier and more confident. Anytime someone can do that for another person, it helps to make the world a better place.

"Weakness of attitude becomes weakness of character." – Albert Einstein

Valuing Your Time

Have you ever thought about how much, or how little, you actually value your time? Do you just give it away here and there not paying much attention to what it is that you are doing with it? Perhaps you spend a lot of time doing things that could easily be done by someone else, instead of freeing up your time to put your talents to better use.

It's crucial that you value your time and know what it is worth. Think about it for a moment – what do you think your time is worth? Is it more valuable than, say, doing the filing in your office? How about more important than checking the stock of office supplies and placing an order? There is a good chance that you believe that your time is more valuable than some of these things. Yet there is a good chance that you are actually doing some of them, too.

Understanding the value of your time is important if you are to have good time management skills. And if you want to run a successful orthodontics or dental practice, you have to have good time management skills. It's a must, so that you can plan accordingly and fit in as many patients as your time will allow. Being good at time management also means you will spend your time doing only the tasks that you should be doing, rather than those you should be delegating to someone else.

Since we are taking a look at the amount of time you spend doing things that could be spent doing better things, let's look at that in the context of how your office actually runs. You may have not even been aware of it at this point, but your staff will suck the time right out of your day. I don't say this to be mean or suggest you should become a mean doctor who doesn't want to speak with anyone in the office. But let's just consider for a moment why it happens in the first place. And here's a hint – it's not their fault.

That's right. Most doctors have not taken the time to properly train their staff. Instead, most of them micro-manage their staff to the point that they are afraid to do anything without the doctor's approval. As you read this, you may be shaking your head in agreement, wondering how you ever hired such incompetent people. Well, there is a really good chance you didn't. Closer to the truth is that you likely hired competent and capable people, and then instead of letting them put their skills to use, you held their hand and taught them to be reliant upon your every move.

It's really not their fault. It's not yours either, because you didn't even realize that what you were doing was causing this problem. But now that you are, you will need to either keep letting things be as they are and maintain the status quo, or you can turn it around and create an office that runs like a well-oiled machine. All you do is stop by once in a while to look in on the oil level and marvel at how well it is all running. The choice really is yours to make.

"Coming together is a beginning. Keeping together is progress. Working together is success." – Henry Ford

MAKING CHANGES

When it comes to doctors micro-managing their offices, you would be surprised at just how much they do. You may even do it a lot more than you realize it or are willing to admit. Since I spend time coaching other doctors, I have gotten to see a lot of ways over the years that doctors are wasting their time. Case in point: we purchased a practice and as we were learning everything about it, we found out that the doctor honestly thought that if he wasn't the one to replace the toilet paper in the restrooms that it would never get done.

You may be thinking "that's crazy," or "not me," but my bet is that there are things along those lines that you are also doing. The bottom line is that the doctor making sure the toilet paper gets stocked regularly in the restroom is not only devaluing his time, but it shouts to the others in the office that you believe them to be incapable of such a minor task. Is that the kind of team and atmosphere you want? If you want a successful practice, you will have to make some changes, starting with your mindset.

MIRROR TIME

While it may be difficult to think about it, the truth is that people often get what they deserve and what they put into it. If you are stocking the toilet paper in your practice's restrooms at 7 p.m. or straightening up the lobby before you head home each night, you have nobody to blame but yourself. I know that is hard to hear. Sometimes the most difficult thing we can do is to recognize where we are going wrong and then to take the steps to make changes. When we do, the payoff is well worth the efforts.

If you are going to have a successful practice that thrives, it is crucial that you learn to delegate. And trust me, I know how difficult that can be for a lot of people. It is hard to let go of the idea that if you want something done right, you have to do it yourself. But with that type of philosophy, you will go home late each night, frustrated and defeated, and will spend the next 10 years spinning your wheels.

Instead, learn to empower your staff. You start by hiring the right people so that you know they are qualified to do what you need them to do, or can easily be trained to do the tasks. Believe me when I say that your staff wants more from you than just money. They want to feel a sense of purpose, like they are contributing to a greater cause, and that they matter. I know this for a fact because I have helped our clients hire and train thousands of employees all over the country, and we have surveyed them. Time and again, the results come back the same – staff members want to contribute, help you grow, take on more responsibility, and feel that what they do makes a difference in your office. Stop turning away from that and let them!

"A real decision is measured by the fact that you've taken a new action. If there's no action, you haven't truly decided." – Tony Robbins

People always think they don't have the time for this or for that. A lack of time is probably the most popular excuse for things like not exercising regularly, reading a new novel, or doing any number of other things. What it really boils down to is that we have all the time in the world for that which we really value.

I've observed in my life that the things I really value always find a room in my budget to get paid. It's probably the same with you and your family. If you disagree with this statement, take a drive around a trailer park. Take notice of all the trailers you will see with satellite dishes. They are on nearly all of the mobile homes. You will also meet parents who complain about the cost of a dental or orthodontic procedure, while later that week they purchase a new iPhone, or they take out a loan for a motorcycle or jet-ski.

Truth be told, people will always find ways to pay for what they value. When it comes to the field we are in, it is our job to help them see the value. Ask yourself what it is that you are doing to increase your value with the services and products you provide to your patients.

When you can explain that and show the value, you will help others to recognize it as well. When that happens, you can expect that your patient list will also grow as a result.

It all comes down to value. You must value your time, what you do with it, and what your services do for others. Then you need to convey that message to others so they understand the value as well and opt for it, rather than investing in the latest video game system for their child.

[11]

Take Action to Shed Excess Baggage and Discover New Capabilities

Dan S. Kennedy

IN THE NOVEL, *Line of Duty*, author Michael Grant has one of his characters deliver this: "A guy I fish with once told me a funny story. He'd just bought an anchor, and as he went forward to tie it to the anchor line, he slipped and fell overboard. Suddenly, he's sitting on the bottom of the lake in fifteen feet of water, cradling his brand new anchor. He didn't want to let go, but he was running out of breath. Realizing his choice was drowning or losing the anchor, he reluctantly let go and swam to the surface." The character in the novel, a police detective, went on to say: "The job has been my anchor and I've been holding on to it for 23 years. I don't want to let go either, but I've run out of breath."

Most people can be caught holding onto prized anchors.

Another way to look at it is in terms of roles. A person gets so used to a role, so comfortable in that role that, even though unhappy, the fear and trauma of stepping outside the role feels worse than the pain of continuing in it. Such roles include: The Victim (why me – it's so unfair), The Martyr (I gave up everything for you), The Last Angry Man (I'm mad as hell at everybody and everything – but I will keep taking it), The Misunderstood Genius, and so on.

So much of our current thoughts and actions have their basis in childhood. My aversion to having a large house with a yard to care for is the direct result of growing up in over-large homes where there was always some damned thing in need of repair or cleaning or replacement, some project to be done or, worse, some disaster to be battled – like, in our second house, a basement that flooded every spring to such a degree that the neighborhood's animals lined up two by two outside. And growing up with yards always in need of mowing or weeding (until I discovered that a hungry Shetland pony on a tether made lawn mowers obsolete). Anyway, I am emotionally averse to all that. Of course, that's obvious. No need for years of therapy to figure that out. And it's not particularly important. But it is only one of who knows how many examples of today's thoughts, attitudes, likes, dislikes, fears, ideas, and behaviors firmly rooted in childhood programming that have never been challenged or even re-considered.

In cases where this does no harm, or even helps, I suppose there's no need to tinker with it. But what about the baggage that does burden, the anchor that does drown, the past programming that does limit? It is plain as can be that people are controlled – yes, controlled – throughout their adult lives by limits that were set and by behaviors that were prescribed early on, then never challenged.

If you are not achieving the results you tell yourself you want out of life, it may very well be that these set-in-the-past restrictions are getting in your way. In the late 1980s, I had the privilege of editing and assembling a new audio program featuring the recorded radio broadcasts and lectures of Dr. Maxwell Maltz, famous in the 1950s for his best-selling book, *Psycho-Cybernetics*, in which he advanced the idea that everything from a person's financial success to the accuracy of his golf swing was controlled by a subconsciously held, very detailed self-image, largely constructed out of childhood programming and experiences, then reinforced through self-talk. Dr. Maltz was first pointed in this direction while in practice as a cosmetic surgeon; many patients came believing that getting some physical flaw fixed – a nose bobbed, breasts enlarged – would alter the way they felt about themselves and make them happier, but even after surgery that made them beautiful or handsome on the outside, they still thought, talked, and acted as if nothing had changed. From this observation, Dr. Maltz made the giant leap – now virtually accepted as universal truth – that a person can practice the perfect golf swing, for example, all he wants and still suffer an awesome slice, unless and until he somehow alters the image he has of himself as a golfer.

There is a kind of mental magnetism connected to the self-image. Earl Nightingale put it this way: we become what we think about most. Of course, that's not instantly, literally true; if it were, as a teenager I'd have become Playmate of the Month. But, over time, it is true. People do think themselves sick. Or old before their time. Or a victim. A perpetual loser.

Certainly, experience alters the self-image. For years, a person considers himself hopelessly clumsy. Then, out of dire necessity, he picks up tools and fixes something and is shocked to discover the awkward lack of coordination of teenage years has been replaced by reasonable facility, and he can drive a nail, and now has to question the long-held, limiting self-image: hey, wait a minute, maybe I'm not so clumsy after all.

There's no reason that has to happen only by happy accident. Instead, you can benefit enormously by testing your limits. "Let's just see if this is still true." The more of this you do, the more likely you are to uncover abilities you didn't know you had.

In *The Hobbit*, Bilbo Baggins said, "I don't like adventures. They make one late for dinner." That is the attitude of far too many people. At age 25, David Smith – college dropout, gambler, playboy, occasional saloonkeeper, began what he has called a "healing journey of exploration." By the time he was 35, he had become the first person to swim from Africa to Europe, had kayaked 2,000 miles down the Nile, run a marathon with tribesmen in Kenya, and put himself through a number of other incredible adventures. (You can read about his story in his book, *Healing Journey: The Odyssey of an Uncommon Athlete*, published by Sierra Club Books.) David inscribed the book to me, "to a man who knows the art of adventure." Frankly, I wish that were a bit truer than it actually is. But I do stretch. I do test. Constantly. Why not? Fortunately, I grew up hearing "How do you know until you try?" You don't.

TAKE A CLOSER LOOK AT THE LABELS SEWN ON YOU

Labels get sewn on children – then they often stay on them as they become adults, even though they are no longer correct (if they ever were). Consider these labels:

- Such a clumsy and awkward child
- Slow learner
- Bookworm
- Shy wallflower...the quiet type
- Daydreamer
- Just not good with _____
  (math; spelling; sports, etc.)

Or consider these: Clint Eastwood was told by an executive at Universal Pictures that he "had no future as an actor" because he had a chipped tooth, an Adams apple that was too prominent, and talked too slow. Best-selling, millionaire author Scott Turow (*Presumed Innocent*) must be a shock to his high school English teacher; Scott got an "F" in that course. In his first fight, Joe Louis was knocked down six times in three rounds, and labeled by one sportswriter as a "doormat with no future." Charles Schultz, creator of "Peanuts", was turned down for a job as a cartoonist at the Disney Studios, and told he "lacked talent".

What Life's Winners Do about Their Labels: The Artichoke Factor

The labels of football teams are interesting. In many cases, there are images invoked for the players to live up to. The Los Angeles Raiders, for example, with the pirate logo, silver and black colors, and "Raiders" name – all that calls for a very tough, aggressive, physical style of play. Players have talked about there being something "special" about that tradition; they've said that when you put on a Raiders uniform, something happens to you inside. For years, the Pittsburgh Steelers were famous for their "Steel Curtain Defense." For obvious reasons, you'll probably never see a football team named "The Williamsburg Librarians."

Which brings us to the small Scottsdale Community College, in 1975, with a very liberal student body opposed to competitive sports. They considered football frivolous, superficial, and representative of a too-violent, too-male-dominated society. As a symbol of their feelings, they elected the artichoke as the official mascot of the college's football team. Imagine the ridicule you'd suffer suiting up and taking the field as a player on The Scottsdale Artichokes!

The Artichokes played their games at a local high school, because their own practice field had no bleachers, and no funds were ever approved for any. Their head coach, John Aviantos, had no scholarships to offer in recruiting talented players. Burdened with the Artichoke name, given no recruiting tools and only minimal funds, Coach Aviantos still won four conference championships, went to two bowl games, and never had a losing season. Coach Aviantos coined the term "The Artichoke Factor" to represent the aspect of a person's character that inspires him to rise to a challenge, to look at the labels that have been sewn on, disagree, and tear them off. "Successful people rarely start out labeled as most-likely-to-succeed," Coach told me. In the sixth year of his tenure there, an 8-foot-high sculpture of an artichoke was erected – a monument to Aviantos' determination not to let a negative, humiliating label stay sewn on his football program and his players.

LABELS SEWN ON "ACCIDENTALLY" IN CHILDHOOD ARE ONE THING – LABELS ATTACHED TO US AS ADULTS ARE ANOTHER

The CBS news anchor Dan Rather once commented that one of the most shocking lessons in life is the discovery that not everyone wishes you well. There is a surprising amount of jealousy, envy, and resentment directed at high achievers in every field. The more you try to do and the more you do, the more you will be subject to it.

The "Idiot" label has been hastily sewn on many people by a critical media, including President Ronald Reagan, Vice-President Dan Quayle, and more recently, Governor Sarah Palin. Every time this is done, considerable accomplishment that contradicts the label is ignored – why let facts get in the way? Tom Monaghan, the original founder and developer of Domino's Pizza, once commented about how easily and quickly he went from being "boy genius" to "village idiot." Once, while engaged in a complex consulting project for a large, troubled corporation – for which I was being paid a million dollars – I asked for the list of their franchisees to review and choose some to personally interview. The list I was given included a former CEO of the company, long retired, who had a single store in a small town to, as they put it, piddle around with. The current corporate leaders made it clear they thought this guy of no current relevance – basically, an idiot. I found him to be far saner than the present management team, and afterward, suggested they cancel my contract and hire him to right the ship.

Most of the severest, most persistent, most sarcastic and mocking critics of Reagan, Quayle, and Palin have never been asked by either political party to run as President or Vice-President, never campaigned for and won a Senate seat or state Governor's office or served in the White House. The vast majority of critics are people of little accomplishment. There has only been one movie critic in history to ever write and produce a movie – and it was a terrible flop – yet he routinely labeled writers, producers, actors and movie executives idiots. Labeling others is easy. Accomplishment, not so easy.

At one time or another, you, too, may be labeled as an idiot. Because I am a firm, consistent, cautionary, and critical voice to entrepreneurs about surrendering to the tyranny of technology, to peer pressure about its use, to popular but not necessarily deserving of investment online media, and because I famously refuse to carry a cell-phone or personally use the internet, I know well that I am viewed and gossiped about as a dinosaurish idiot by many – despite a growing body of evidence that people's productivity is often severely impaired by their indiscriminate adoption of each and every new social media activity and gadget, and despite a growing "underground" of top CEOs and business leaders and authors opting out. What others think of me is really unimportant to me, to the point that my profound disinterest in their approval or disapproval makes them very unhappy. In an earlier chapter, I spoke of the success-store's non-negotiable price tags. It's my experience that one of these price tags is being willing to be thought of poorly, one way or another, by many.

The "Washed Up Has-Been" label was sewn on Joan Rivers after the loss of her talk show and the suicide of her husband, and it was sewn on by her own agent and manager, many supposed friends, and the media. Joan defied the label with grit, hard work, a willingness to go through any door of opportunity she could find, humor, talent and self-confidence. She refused to let her actions be limited or dictated by the label others were so eager to attach to her.

In preparation for another book, I did considerable research on Debbi Fields, founder of Mrs. Fields Cookies. She and I also appeared as speakers on several events together. Debbie is arguably one of the best known, most widely recognized, and most phenomenally successful women entrepreneurs of our time. But in the beginning she was labeled as an "empty-headed housewife" by her husband's business acquaintances, bankers, family, "friends," vendors, and suppliers.

Fran Tarkenton, whom I've gotten to know thanks to a number of Guthy-Renker Corporation projects, was labeled "too small to play in the NFL." Today's quarterbacks are still scrambling to catch up to some of his records. Doug Flutie, a collegiate football superstar, was labeled "too small" to play pro ball by the NFL. One year he was the most valuable player – with his multi-million dollar arm – in the expanding Canadian Football League.

It seems that the world is eager to attach labels; too old...too young...too small...too big...too slow...too dumb...too clumsy...too inexperienced...too this-or-that. You've just about got to keep one eye open while you sleep because somebody may be sneaking up to try and label you.

It is important to note that successful people tend to defy their labels past and present with their actions. Unsuccessful people accept and conform to their labels, by their actions.

Take Action to Win Over Worry

Dan S. Kennedy

I HAVE HAD a great many misfortunes in my life – but only about half as many as I have painfully anticipated.

Worry can create physical illnesses, stress and fatigue. Worry robs you of your competence and confidence. Many people are literally immobilized by worry.

Yet, as destructive as we know worry to be, and as unnecessary as worrying often proves to be, most people still let worry into their lives virtually every day. Ironically, we give our worries power by thinking about them. The more you worry about something, the more power worry itself gains over you. Even small worries can amass enormous power if you let them. Dr. Edward Kramer observed: "A penny held to the eye blocks the sun."

So, how do you eliminate worry from your life?

I'm not sure you can eliminate it. Worry is often the starting point of constructive, creative thought. But you can reduce its time consumption and influence in your life.

You can temporarily do it with chemicals. Booze. Prescription, over-the-counter, or street drugs. Personally, I used the drink-to-coma method myself, for several years. The problem with that is, when you return to the real world, the things you were worrying about are there waiting for you, and you're further handicapped in dealing with them by the hangovers and other physical debilitation. This kind of escape yields no real benefit and has its own added costs. I can't speak to the drug thing, as I've never tried any street drugs and very rarely even swallow a Tylenol. But I can talk about alcohol from experience, and I'll only briefly say this: if you find yourself knocking back a few every day, everything you tell yourself about not having a problem is crap. You've got a problem. *Not* a solution; a problem. If you protect it and continue with it, it will eventually destroy your business or career, an important relationship, your health, or land you in jail. If you cannot quickly kick this habit alone, get help.

The only real antidote for worry is action.

Decision is the empowering opposite of worry. When you take action to solve a problem, you take power away from the problem, and you gain power. For every source of worry and anxiety, there is usually a list of a number of potentially helpful actions. If you'll get involved in making that list and acting on all the items on the list, worry will be eliminated; it cannot co-exist with such constructive action.

I recently read an article about a CEO of a huge company, on the brink of financial ruin, presented with the fact that they had only enough cash to operate the business for another three days. "What then," he asked, "are we going to spend it on?" He was instantly moving on to actions, not worry.

If you find yourself too frequently immobilized by worry, I have a book to recommend: W. Clement Stone's *The Success System That Never Fails*. Pay particular attention to his discussion of the sudden termination of his right to represent a particular company; the end of a business he had struggled mightily to build; an eminent and apparently unmanageable threat to everything he had and everything he had worked for; and how he reacted to it.

But – what about the problem you cannot take any action to resolve? First of all, there's rarely any situation that defies all action. But, for the sake of conversation, let's assume that you are up against something so tough that, at least at the moment, there is absolutely nothing you can do, no action you can take. If that is the case, then the only thing you can do is set that problem aside entirely and take action on some other matter or project that you can do something about.

The *only* antidote for worry is action.

What about worrying about what others think? A great deal of unhappiness comes from people pursuing and achieving others' goals instead of their own. When I was a kid, one of our neighbors, Ralph F., created a great deal of unhappiness for himself, his wife, and his five sons by obsessing over his sons' disinterest in taking over the family business. I wonder how many kids buckle under to such pressure and achieve the goals their parents' set for them – and wind up wishing they hadn't. Working to achieve others' goals set for you, to meet others' expectations, to satisfy others' definitions, that is what you do when you worry about what others think.

My friend, the late Herb True, had moved from the academic world to a very successful career in professional speaking, and could have continued to enjoy a growing, exceptional income, create and market cassette albums, author best-selling books and accumulate wealth. He chose not to. Herb chose to cut his business back to taking just a few speaking engagements a year so he could return to teaching at Notre Dame. When he did so, I know that many of his peers and friends thought he'd lost his marbles. Or gotten too old to compete. Or had the business pass him buy. None of those things were true. But regardless of what anybody else or everybody else thought, Herb chose to pursue his goals. The result was one of the most contented but invigorated, happy and fulfilled individuals I know or have ever observed.

Oh, and you'd probably be surprised (disappointed?) if you knew how little others think about you. Most people have their hands full dealing with their own lives. They ponder yours a lot less than you probably assume. But regardless of how little or great the world's interest is in how you choose to live your life, "sooner or later you stand in your own space." The cure for worry over others' opinions is taking action that satisfies you and, as a result, increases your sense of control, feeling of power, self-confidence, and self-esteem. Others can never gift you with self-esteem or peace of mind. These are products of your own actions.

[13]

Take Action to Conquer Your Fears

Dustin S. Burleson

IF YOU ARE like most of the doctors whom I have worked with in coaching, I would bet you spend a lot of time worrying. You think about this, think about that, and meanwhile nothing positive happens. Instead you spin your wheels. You go nowhere, which tends to leave you frustrated, exhausted, and unsure of what to do and where to turn. Trust me when I say there is a better way.

That better way focuses around actually taking action. When we consistently spend our time thinking about things, worrying or trying to decide, we are paralyzed and get nowhere. It's only when we take action that we come alive. I know you are worried about taking the wrong action. But even if sometimes it turns out to be the wrong action, at least you will have realized that and can make another change. Sometimes we have to head down a dead-end street before we realize that we turned down the wrong road. When that happens, we simply turn around and get going down the right path. But just the act of having taken the action in the first place got us moving and started making things happening.

> *"Happiness is not something ready made. It comes from your own actions."*
> *– Dalai Lama*

FACT FINDING

When you think about it, you will agree with me when I say that doctors are heavy fact-finders, and as a result we experience analysis paralysis. This is why we don't change our office décor for 30 years. It's why we can never make the decision to expand our practice. It's the reason we will dilly-dally trying to decide if we need additional employees to serve our patients better.

No matter what it is, fill in the blank, you know you get stuck with over-analyzing things. You take something that could be simple and you fact check it to the point of exhaustion. You mull it over until your brain hurts. Meanwhile nothing gets done. You may stay that way for weeks, months, or even years. And when that happens you are in a state of paralysis where your business will not grow. Nothing will.

It's only once you take action that you free yourself from the hold these issues have on you. Think of them as chains that are holding you back from reaching your goal or destination. The sooner you break free of those chains, the faster you will be heading down the path toward your goals. I'm not saying you should not think about anything and consider the facts. But what

I am saying is that you may be over-thinking small issues to the extreme. Think about it, consider, make a decision, and move on.

Keep taking action. That is the only way you can keep your practice growing. You must stay active, rather than being paralyzed by inaction.

Do you remember when you were studying for your board exams? Sure you do! But think about it, you could go sick just from worrying about the exams. In fact, you would worry until you finally just sat down at the desk, cracked open the books, and began studying. Right? Once you took action, the worry just kind of melted away. That's because taking action is the number one cure for worry in your practice, creating hiring and training systems, remodeling the office, expanding your hours, offering new services, and so on. These are all things that have absolutely crippled my clients, and I'm sad to say that I've witnessed firsthand things gobbling up years of our clients' time. Once they get started moving the ball forward, they called me laughing at how easy it was and how they can't imagine (years later) that they would ever have spent time worrying about something so trivial, especially when they see the results that have been produced.

It's difficult to imagine that you will also feel that these things that have you worrying will at some point seem trivial but, believe me, they will. Taking action when you are not used to taking action can seem overwhelming at first. But once you do it, you begin to see that you feel better, freer, and in more control than ever before. It also becomes easier once you begin doing it on a regular basis.

> *"If you want to conquer fear, don't sit home and think about it. Go out and get busy." – Dale Carnegie*

SIZING UP RETURNS

Take a few minutes to consider the best decisions you have made for your practice, as well as your best returns on investment. What might your practice look like today had you actually made the decision years ago?

Taking action means you can reap the rewards of those decisions and actions now.

It is important to note again that you may not always make the right decision. Whatever you do, don't let that make you afraid to make some decisions and take action. When you are in the habit of taking massive action, you will have the ability to quickly navigate the choppy waters of practice. Think of it in terms of a large barge or transport ship that is heading in one direction. This is what your practice is like when you spend your time worrying. You end up staying on one, long slow path. When you finally make a decision to adapt, turn around, and change something, you take a long time to do it.

When you are accustomed to rapid change, and rapid action, however, you are like a jet-ski or small powerboat that can quickly crisscross back and forth over the water. You can adapt quickly, change directions at a moment's notice, and you can get back to shore more quickly and refuel as needed.

As you can see, it just makes sense that leaving the worry behind and being able to move freely is going to help you accomplish more. Your options will be greater and your agility will be far superior. Get in the habit of taking action. Quite honestly, it is the only way to get things done, instill change, and reach those goals you have set.

BOARD DECISIONS

Just like when you would worry for board exams and it would hold you back, the same goes on with your practice today. When you sat down and got started studying, you realized that things were not as scary as they may have seemed. When you decide to take action with your practice, you will see that you shouldn't have spent so much time worrying there, either. All that worry and fear prevents you from growing and reaching your goals. Make the decision today that fear will not hold you back any longer, and then begin taking action right now.

"In order to succeed, your desire for success should be greater than your fear of failure." – Bill Cosby

OVERCOMING FEAR OF FAILURE

Even though you have made it to the point of graduating from dental school and having your own practice, you may have a fear of failure. Many people have a fear of failure that keeps them from reaching their full potential. By overcoming that fear, you will be able to reach your goals and have the level of success with your practice that you desire. Here are 8 tips for helping you overcome the fear of failure:

1. Come to terms with the fact that you have a fear of failure and that your worry is holding you back. Once you realize it, you can begin to do something about it.

2. Think about the missed opportunities and goals you may not reach if you continue with the status quo and do not take action.

3. Determine the goals you want to reach. Make a list of them, whether they are two weeks from now or two years from now. Write down the goals you want to accomplish.

4. Create a list of milestones that you can take to reach each of the goals that you have set. Make the milestones something you can measure, so that you know if you have made progress toward them.

5. Set your fears and worry aside and dive right in. Get active working toward reaching the goals you have chosen.

6. Think positively. Make a pact with yourself to focus on the positives and not the possibilities of what can go wrong. Envision the success you want.

7. Consistently work toward the goals, and every time fear creeps into your mind, revert back to the positive thoughts to push it out.

8. If challenges arise, just focus on solutions. The same goes for setbacks. Keep moving forward, taking action in order to get closer to the success you want.

[14]

Take Action When Your "Inner Voice" Speaks

DAN S. KENNEDY

ABOUT 50 YEARS ago or so, an expectant mother took a $500.00 risk and placed a little ad in *Seventeen* for a new purse monogrammed with the customer's initials. She believed in her idea and acted on it, even though $500.00 was a great deal of money for her at the time, even though she had no market research to support it, even though she had no business experience. Her little ad produced $32,000.00 in orders. The Lillian Vernon

Company matured to selling more than 150 million dollars of merchandise every year, ultimately sold for a queenly price.

In a speech to the New York Venture group on May 17, 1990, Lillian Vernon said, "I make quick decisions. I take chances, relying on what I consider 'my golden gut.'"

She went on to say: "Growing from a million dollar to a multi-million dollar company involved areas such as finance, list management, computers, and large-scale production realms beyond my expertise. I tried to cover my shortcomings by surrounding myself with experienced veterans of large corporate cultures, usually from outside the direct marketing industry. There were so few direct marketers in the early 1970s that I filled my ranks with managers from different walks of life who generally were very savvy to the ways of big business – and most of them almost killed us. I don't want to generalize, but some of the corporate executives I hired just couldn't make a decision. They took analysis to the point of paralysis. Every consideration had to first be studied by a committee. In my business, sending a good idea to a committee is like sending Rip Van Winkle to a slumber party. I hate more than anything to wake up and find that one of my competitors is already doing something I was planning on." For many years, Lillian Vernon continued picking winning products for her catalogs, often trusting her "golden gut" and making fast decisions. Other great mail-order catalog merchants, including my friend Joe Sugarman, J. Peterman – made famous in the Seinfeld TV shows as Elaine's boss, and featured in my book, *No B.S. Marketing to the Affluent*, and Roger Horchow have these two things in common: the knack for spotting a promotable product and the trust in their own intuition and instincts to act. Without the second thing, the first wouldn't be of much value.

Confident decisiveness is one of the most prized qualities in the business world. All great leaders exhibit it. People naturally respond to such a person. It is easy for the decisive individual to inspire trust and cooperation. Where does this kind of confident decisiveness come from? Call it what you will:

intuition, the golden gut, the inner voice, insight – most exceptionally successful people admit to listening to a secret, inner advisor.

A FEW THOUGHTS ABOUT INSIGHT

> *"The mind can only proceed so far upon what it knows, and can prove. There comes a point where the mind takes a leap – call it intuition or what you will – and comes out on a higher plane of knowledge." – Albert Einstein*

My friend and speaking colleague Lee Milteer wrote an outstanding book, *Success Is An Inside Job*, and I thought excerpts from its chapter on "Intuition: Your Secret Talent" would be appropriate here:

"It is interesting that in our western culture we seem to comprehend almost all of our experiences through the logical, linear, analytical thinking process. We use words to communicate this kind of thinking. Because words are our way of understanding our world, we've almost forgotten we have an intuitive, creative part of ourselves. We're not trained to say *I feel* but rather *I think*. If we deny and cut off our intuition, then we get trapped by concepts learned through our programmed minds. Yesterday's learned beliefs (alone) cannot solve today's challenges or enable us to capitalize on tomorrow's opportunities."

Today more and more successful people – executives, artists, entrepreneurs – are realizing that making decisions is not an exclusive function of the analytical left side of the brain. You must now use the intuitive and creative right side of your brain as well. You must have an integration of analytical and intuitive thinking. This is commonly referred to as "whole brain thinking." Dr. Jonas Salk said, "A new way of thinking is now needed to deal with our present reality. Our subjective responses (intuitive) are more sensitive and more rapid than our objective responses (reasoned). This is the nature of the way the mind works. We first sense, then we reason why."

I suggest that you have some fun in your life and start testing your intuitive abilities. When the phone rings, ask yourself who it is before you answer – see how many times you're right. When waiting for an elevator, guess which one will come first. There are dozens of small games you can play with yourself to strengthen your abilities. Your "intuitive muscle" gets stronger as you use it. Then, when you need your intuition, you will feel more confident in using it.

In his book *The Intuitive Edge*, Philip Goldberg noted the "......astonishing speed with which the truly intuitive mind can bring together bits of information only remotely related in time and meaning to form the sudden hunch or whispered feeling that we call intuition." Conrad Hilton, who was well known for using his intuition in his hotel business, wrote "I know when I have a problem and have done all I can to figure it out. I keep listening in a sort of inside silence till something clicks and I feel a right answer.'"

Here are some of Lee's action tips for encouraging your intuition:

- Listen to your body; that's why we call intuition a 'gut' feeling. The solar plexus is a large network of nerves located behind the stomach and is said to be the seat of emotion. You can have an accurate, gut-level reaction to many situations.

- Allow yourself to re-define the problem frequently; writing out the problem gives you the opportunity to see the problem from a different perspective.

- Allow yourself to play. You don't have to be sitting in your office to come up with creative and intuitive solutions. Take a walk, feed the birds, play hooky for an hour and then come back to work on the problem.

- Take action on your insights. Start investigating with the approach of "will this hunch logically work?"

Two of the self-help pioneers that I've long been a serious student of, Napoleon Hill and Dr. Edward Kramer, both promote reliance on insight and intuition. I don't often talk about it, but I often act on little flashes that come to me seemingly out of the blue. I'll give you an example:

Some years back, at a seminar about direct marketing where I was a featured speaker, one of the attendees was a long-time subscriber and student of mine, a chiropractor in private practice, and the owner of a practice management company consulting with other doctors. During the two days, I heard him talk about his goals for expanding his second business. On the flight home, a flash came – I'll bet he would buy my SuccessTrak business, centered around my *Practice-Building Secrets* newsletter for chiropractors. Prior to that flash, I had not been thinking about selling that business, although I was gradually recognizing that it was no longer a good fit with my other interests and activities, was being neglected, and was losing value. As I thought about this flash, I developed the argument in my mind for the synergy between this doctor's management business and goals and why my business would be worth more to him than to me. Most importantly – let me say it again: most importantly, immediately on my arrival at home, I generated a letter to him suggesting the deal. It was consummated to my satisfaction in a matter of weeks.

For me, this is not at all unusual. These flashes frequently occur, I frequently act on them quickly, and I frequently benefit as a result. Consequently, I'm a believer in the role of intuition in otherwise hard-nosed, tough-minded, pragmatic business environments. And I find information on the subject, such as that Lee has assembled in her book, of great value.

(You can find information about Lee's books at leemilteer.com)

How to Use the Miraculous "Dominant Thought Principle" to Energize Your Inner Advisor

I will try to tell this true-life story as briefly as possible: in my hometown of Akron, Ohio, a prominent judge, a respected citizen, a family man, wound up on the front page of The Akron Beacon Journal and in prison as a child molester. This was more than 30 years ago; we were still shocked by such things. He was asked how a man like him could wind up in such a horrible situation. He described a process – he said, "One day, years ago, I was out watering my lawn, a little girl in a sundress went by and for a fleeting millisecond I thought about what it would be like with her – then, of course, I pushed it from my mind. But a year or so later, at a mall, another little girl, and I held the thought for maybe a minute." He went on to mention another incident, a few minutes of thought. Another incident, 15 or 20 minutes of thought. "Then one day," he said, "I woke up and found it was all I was thinking about. For days, it dominated my thoughts. Then I did it."

This is a *negative* example of the amazing power of Dominant Thought.

After 20 years of intense research into what made super successful people tick, Napoleon Hill wrote: "Our brains become magnetized with the dominating thoughts which we hold in our minds, and by means with which no man is familiar, these magnets attract to us the forces, the people, the circumstances of life which harmonize with the nature of our dominating thoughts."

I know this to be true, personally, in its positive and its negative application.

When you come to grips with this Dominant Thought Principle, you have the supercharger device for dramatically accelerating the achievement of any objective; instead of taking weeks, months or years to move from first, fleeting thought to dominant thought, deliberately utilize dominant thought --- because the lapse of time between dominant thought, action, and achievement is minimal. All the time is taken up in getting to dominant thought. Very little time is required to get from dominant thought to reality.

Beyond this, dominant thoughts energize your Inner Advisor. Your dominant thoughts are your Inner Advisor's directives. Your dominant thoughts tell your Inner Advisor what to work on. Your Inner Advisor then jumps into action; mobilizes all the vast resources of your subconscious mind, your memory, your experience, your connection to universal intelligence. Then your Inner Advisor tells you precisely what to do, who to call, where to go and when to act, to get from dominant thought to reality as rapidly as possible. When you energize your Inner Advisor with deliberate dominant thought, you can trust and confidently, decisively act on the Advisor's recommendations.

[15]

Take Action to Manifest Your Dreams

Dustin S. Burleson

YOU MAY NOT be familiar with the term "Laws of Attraction," but that is what is at work when you apply the Dominant Thought principle discussed in the prior chapter. The Laws of Attraction follow a simple principle: what you think about is what is brought to you. It's a concept that has been around for a long time and is used by many successful people around the world.

Napoleon Hill wrote about it in his famous *Think and Grow Rich* book. The concept, although having various names, was around even before he penned that book in 1937. In recent years, the same concept has been successfully re-hashed in the best-selling book called *The Secret*. While the names of the books and concept may vary, the basic idea remains the same. If you want success, you have to think success. If your mind is thinking of all the negatives, then you will continue to get more negatives. That's because your dominant thought is that of something negative. Whatever it is that is dominating your thoughts is what is going to become a reality. That's why it's important to focus on positive thoughts about how you want a successful practice.

In other words, focus your mind on what it is that you do want, not on what it is that you don't want. Whatever it is your mind is focusing on, whether positive or negative, what you want or don't want, is what is going to be attracted to you and become your reality.

"Patience, persistence and perspiration make an unbeatable combination for success." – Napoleon Hill

SOLUTIONS APPEAR

When it comes to trusting your intuition, you will find that the solutions to some of your challenges will automatically appear. Perhaps you don't see them immediately, so you are a little skeptical. But they do indeed appear, it's just that the solutions appear when you are prepared to see them and are prepared to receive them.

If the solutions appeared to you when you were not ready for them, or at a point where you were not willing to receive them, they would be of no value. You would simply overlook them, put them out of your mind, or brush them off as something other than the solution you are looking for. But when you are ready and they appear, you will embrace them and have that "ah-ha" moment, so long as you are trusting your intuition.

A funny thing happened to one of my coaching clients that pertains to seeing things when you are ready for them. One of my clients needed to expand, and it was time that she finally take steps to do so. This was after years of delaying an expansion in which she would need a new building for her practice. One day, she called me, filled with excitement in her voice, announcing that "You're not going to believe this, but there is a building right across the street from me that is perfect and it is available!"

"Yes," I told her. "It's been empty and for lease for the last five years. You just weren't prepared to see it as an option. Either your inner voice wasn't ready yet or you weren't listening to it."

Chances are, you have experienced something similar at one point or another. You may have just not been all that in touch with what was going on. But make no mistake, when you are ready to see and accept the solutions to your challenges, they will be right in front of you.

> *"Men are not prisoners of fate, but only prisoners of their own minds."*
> *– Franklin D. Roosevelt*

PUTTING IT INTO ACTION

As a doctor who is reading this book, it is fair to assume that you want a successful practice, or that you want to make your current practice become more successful. Yet you may be spending your days thinking negatively about the things you don't want. You don't want your competitor to get bigger than you. You don't trust your office staff to take on more responsibility. Whatever it is, there is a good chance that your thoughts are focused on those things that you don't want, rather than the things that you do want. What you should be focusing on are all things "successful practice." By doing this, you will be making it known what you would like, and it will begin to move toward you and become a reality.

Once you have the Dominant Thought process working in your favor, you will need to take action. If you don't, all that energy will have been for nothing. When the things come into your path that you have been seeking and wanting, it is essential that you take action. By acting on those things, you will help see them through.

It's not just about thinking positively about what you want. It's about also putting forth the energy to act on those things when they are presented. Do that, and you will succeed.

OVERCOMING NEGATIVITY

Many people think of themselves as negative. I've come across people who believe this both in my coaching and in other areas of my life. They will label themselves as a "pessimist," always assuming the worst, thinking of the negative, and feeling that if something can go wrong it will. You know, the Murphy's Law line of thinking. But that type of thinking, as you are learning, will not get you very far. Yet I know that for many of you it may be difficult to snap your fingers and just change your line of thinking.

Becoming an optimist, or more positive person, is going to take some practice. This is especially true for those who have spent their lives labeling themselves as a pessimist. For starters, start calling yourself an optimist. By changing that label, you will already start to have more positive thoughts enter your mind. Other things you can do to help overcome negativity include:

- Start every morning with a positive thought about what it is that you want to accomplish today.
- Smile more. Even if you are not feeling all that happy or are driving in the car by yourself, just smile for a few minutes. By putting this smile on your face it will make your brain think you are happy, and you will become happier as a result.
- Find others who are positive thinkers, and begin surrounding yourself with them. You have probably heard before that attitudes are catchy, so you want to make sure that you have one worth catching, and that those around you have attitudes worth catching.

- When you begin having negative thoughts, change them. Remind yourself why thinking positively is important and immediately begin changing those thoughts.
- Every day, show gratitude. Whether you keep a gratitude journal, as many people do, or you just announce out loud things you are grateful for it is important to acknowledge all you have that you are grateful for. When you do that, more things to be grateful for will begin moving toward you.
- Find things that inspire you, whether quotes, poetry, or music, and make them a regular part of your life. These things are important in helping you to maintain a healthy attitude.
- Again, stop labeling yourself with negative labels. Those negative labels are not going to help you reach your goals and will bring more negativity your way.

When your inner voice or intuition speaks up, it is time to take notice. As you can see, it can make a big difference. The same goes for making sure that we use the power of positive thinking, or the Dominant Thought Principle, in order to help us achieve what it is that we want. To get the ultimate practice that you are seeking, you need to clear the mind of negative thoughts, focus on what it is that you want, and be ready and willing to accept it when it enters your path.

Take Action to Profit from All the Power of Positive Association

DAN S. KENNEDY

ADVERTISING AGENCY EMPIRE-builder David Ogilvy established a tradition of welcoming new executives with a gift of five wooden dolls, each smaller than the other, one inside the other. When the recipient finally gets to the fifth little doll, the smallest doll, and opens it, he finds this message:

If each of us hires people who are smaller than we are, we shall become a company of dwarfs, but if each of us hires people who are bigger than we are, we shall become a company of giants.

You can certainly take this beyond hiring. If you surround yourself and spend time with people who are "smaller" than you are, you will stay as you are.

Take action to involve smart people in your projects. I am constantly impressed with how my clients, Greg Renker and Bill Guthy of the Guthy-Renker Corporation pull together project teams, invite outside experts and consultants to their company meetings, collect qualified opinions and data, and patiently explore differing viewpoints. They constantly apply Napoleon Hill's "mastermind principle." If you aren't familiar, Guthy-Renker is the most successful producer of TV infomercials, and has used that media and just about every other media to build giant brands and businesses, including Proactiv® acne treatments, which began with a show featuring actress Judith Light, and as I'm writing this revised edition, many years later, has Justin Bieber, Katy Perry and Jennifer-Love Hewitt featured in the advertising. I've worked as a consultant and writer for Guthy-Renker off and on for more than 20 years, and have often been part of a specific project team, as well as a "mastermind participant" engaged in evaluating new product possibilities, devising advertising strategies and themes, and more. They view me as a smart fellow, and I appreciate the 20-year-long compliment.

What's significant about this is that these men, who have built a billion dollar a year enterprise from scratch, have never reached that dangerous pinnacle of arrogance and isolation: thinking they are smarter than everybody else. Making a billion dollars a year can do that to you. But it hasn't done it to them. People of far lesser achievement do fall victim to this syndrome, and often discover that the slide down the back-side of the mountain happens a lot faster than did the climb up.

TAKE A MILLIONAIRE TO LUNCH

There are smart people readily accessible everywhere. You might seek out and tap retired and highly experienced executives or entrepreneurs in your field to assist and advise you. You might find successful people in your field, in other geographic areas, happy to share their experiences for the price of a lunch or dinner. My speaking colleague Jim Rohn urges people: "Take a millionaire to lunch." Jim says to buy him a big juicy steak, fine wine, then dessert, and keep asking him questions, and keep listening carefully. And he observes that most people are too short-sighted to ever take this advice: "Hey, the guy's a millionaire? – let him buy his own steak." I'd add that most people take people to lunch who know less than they do, have less successful experience than they do, like a tennis player preferring the company of inferior players. You might find smart, helpful people through professional associations or at seminars and conferences. You might need to hire smart people to advise you or provide very specialized services for your business. Only one thing is certain; you won't find smart people if you do not take action to find them.

Most highly successful entrepreneurs are, these days, involved in several different formally organized mastermind groups, coaching programs, and networking organizations, and it's likely that the person who put this book in your hands offers one or more such opportunities. There are also local "Dan Kennedy Study Groups" and Chapters meeting in many cities nationwide, accessible via DanKennedy.com, with free guest passes usually available on request. Also, nearly every successful entrepreneur has at least a few key advisors he cheerfully pays to be part of his private brain trust. Even today's pro golfer, who appears to be playing a solo game, is actually very reliant on an expert caddie, swing coach, sports psychologist and, off the course, financial advisor, attorney, licensing and brand management team, and publicist.

There are many good purposes served by such exposure and sharing of ideas and experiences among peers as well as the investing in solid, expert advice – not the least of which is avoiding unnecessary, costly mistakes.

At the American Booksellers Association, I ran into a young couple who had authored and published an excellent, unusual travel book. I had met them about seven months earlier at a conference for self-publishers where I spoke. At that conference, they had asked me a few questions, but been resistant to advice they didn't like, clearly eager for someone to validate their own opinions, and even more clearly unwilling to pay for expert assistance. At this industry conference, they told me of having just appeared on a major national, network daytime talk show. But their book wasn't in stores and they never got their own 800# given out on the show, were not prepared to negotiate that with the show's producers, and were not prepared to hold their own as one of several guests on a panel – another of the guests monopolized the entire show. I certainly could have made sure they got their 800# shown and given out on the show, the calls handled, probably sold 5,000 or more books immediately by phone and collected three times that many inquiries, coached them in asserting themselves on the show, and otherwise helped them capitalize on this very difficult to get exposure. And I'm not the only one; there are any number of people very well qualified as advisors in such a situation. But they squandered a once-in-a-lifetime opportunity by being stubborn and by being cheap.

Every business, every occupation, and every field has grown far too complex for one person to go it alone and capably handle every aspect of the activity. Insisting on doing *everything* yourself is very false economy.

In his first book, Lee Iacocca wrote about his "team of horses" – the mastermind group that turned Chrysler into a winner. In many instances, the existence and importance of a mastermind group within a business or organization goes unnoticed by most of the outside world. But behind most successes, there is between a 2-person and a 20-person mastermind alliance hard at work.

Now, here's a tricky part: you cannot listen only to advice you like and only to opinions that validate your own. Well, you can, but you'll almost certainly fail in most of your endeavors. Sometimes the most valuable person is the one with the courage to confront you and tell you "the Emperor has no clothes."

On the other hand, you need to take great care in choosing those people you test ideas on and solicit opinions from. At my seminars, I all too often hear from the person who had a "great idea," bounced it off a few friends, got talked out of it, only to subsequently see someone else come up with the same idea and go on to amass a fortune. It's a frequently told tale. In describing the proper makeup of a mastermind group – the short list of those people you choose to routinely serve as your sounding boards – Dr. Napoleon Hill wrote: "We share nothing we plan to achieve with anyone except those who believe in us and who are in complete sympathy with our plans." This does not mean "yessers." No, we need good criticism. We need someone to point out the flaws and hazards we may overlook in our enthusiasm. But these people have to be truly eager for our success, confident of our abilities, progressive, innovative and optimistic in general, and possessing of successful, relevant experience and knowledge.

Walt Disney was more brutal and brief in his comments about others' opinions. He would typically ask ten people for their opinions and when all ten disliked one of his ideas he would rate that one as most worthy of investment. The great actor Peter Ustinov said, "If the world should blow itself up tomorrow, the last audible voice would be that of an expert saying: it can't be done."

Beware the expert who can only tell you what you *cannot* do (or cannot do without the expert). Look, instead, for the knowledgeable person who may point out flaws and question premises but can and will also suggest possibilities and improvements and, in general, is eager to figure out how you *can* accomplish your stated objectives.

Such people have to be "big" enough not to be jealous or envious of your success and accomplishments. They have to be smart enough to know what they do not know, and secure enough to admit it – a person with equally strong opinions about everything cannot be trusted. They must not fear the truth or shun reality, but they must be, overall, optimistic and positive-minded by nature. To paraphrase the title of Peter McWilliams' book, you cannot afford the luxury of a truly negative individual as a close advisor. And your collection of advisors should include people from inside your particular field and from other, diverse fields.

Finally, in soliciting and considering opinions, there is a time to say "enough has to be enough" and then take action. I have often taken pains to correct peoples' picture of the entrepreneur as a wild-eyed risk-*taker*, defining the entrepreneur, instead, as someone who *manages* risk. Obviously, the more information and worthwhile opinion you can assemble and consider before making an important decision, the better – however, this balances out against a value-of-passing-time issue...the assembly and evaluation of information can become a never-ending pursuit in and of itself, with always one more person yet to be heard from, one more source yet to consult, one more piece of data to be obtained. If you're constantly seduced by the next piece of information to be uncovered, paralysis of analysis takes over.

THE 3-LEGGED STOOL OF SUCCESSFUL ACHIEVEMENT

Picture in your mind a 3-Legged Stool. If any one leg is missing, you can't sit on it; you topple over. One leg is no more important than the other. All three legs share exactly equal importance. Two without three is no better than one without two or even none. All three are vitally necessary. Their importance is evenly, perfectly balanced.

So, one of these legs is: *information*. Another: *advice and association*. The third is: *decision and action*.

Watch the pro football coach on the sidelines the next time a game is on television. He has less than a minute between plays to direct his offense. He has *information*: in his hands, usually on pages attached to a clipboard, is a game plan, including a collection of planned plays, all built on prior, careful analysis of information collected about the opposing team's strengths, weaknesses, and behavior, as well as his own players' abilities, strengths and weaknesses. He has *advice and association*: during the week before the game, most coaches confer with all their assistant coaches and players, and often by phone with a few trusted, little-mentioned advisors, like other coaches, retired coaches. During the game, he is getting input from assistant coaches in the Skybox above the field and from other assistants on the sidelines with him. He is getting instant feedback from the players – here's what happened...here's what I noticed on the last play. But then he still has less than a minute to arrive at a *decision*. And it doesn't matter whether it is what might be judged as a minimally important situation – the first play of the game – or a life-or-death situation, 4th and 4, two minutes left, down by a touchdown; he still has less than a minute. How would you do under similar pressure?

Of these three legs, *advice and association* is the one you can and need to set up in advance, cultivate over time, and use on a daily basis. You'll do yourself a great favor by organizing your own network, your own brain trust or people whose judgment and support you can depend on. You'll do yourself another favor by joining formal mastermind groups and coaching programs run by reputable experts.

It's important to add that successful people are always *actively* on the lookout for valuable, authentic sources of information, advisors, individuals with useful experience to share, providers of new opportunities and services, and allies who can somehow help them better reach their goals.

This trait exhibits itself in many actions, small and large. Such people do not merely order the occasional book from Amazon called to their attention by somebody else; they frequently visit a large bookstore and wander and browse, to find what they don't know exists, that might benefit them. They occasionally haunt used bookstores for the same purpose. When they attend conferences, they do not skirt the exhibit hall; they diligently search it....they do not hang out only with friends; they actively engage new people....they do not skip sessions...and they routinely invest in offered resources they discover by being there. It is self-serving to point that last thing out, but I've been at this for 35 years, I'll wager the biggest steak in Texas that I intimately know a lot more made-from-scratch millionaire, multi-millionaire and even billionaire entrepreneurs than you do, and I can assure you: they are nearly compulsive buyers of success information.

They also go to pains and spare no expense in getting to the source and securing one-to-one advice and coaching relevant to their objectives. I routinely have very smart and accomplished people flying to meet with me at one of my homes – I never travel to someone's place of business to consult – and, as of this writing, they pay the princely sum of $18,800.00 to sit with me from 9:00 AM to 4:00 PM and pick my brain. And I suspect I could charge more, but I'm not a greedy man. Many do this a couple times every year, year after year. Have I hypnotized or mesmerized them? Not at all. I am not the only beneficiary of their unending, active search for new, for better; their unending, active re-assessment of their own ideas, beliefs and modus operandi. It is their success behavior.

[17]

Take Action to Surround Yourself with Winners

DUSTIN S. BURLESON

IF YOU HAVEN'T given much thought to your closest friends, now is the perfect time to take stock. What many people don't realize is that you will in all likelihood become the average of your three closest friends. If you are like many others, you are drumming up the names and profiles of your three closest friends right now.

While you may have not given it much thought before, it is true that you will become the average of your three closest friends. This extrapolates to every area of your life. You will be the average of your three closest orthodontic friends, three closest church friends, and so on. Because of this, it is important to choose your friends, and business associates, as well as those who you surround yourself with, with care.

"I don't need a friend who changes when I change and who nods when I nod; my shadow does that much better." – Plutarch

MAKING IMPROVEMENTS

Another important question to ask yourself is what you are doing in your professional practice to improve your employees? While you may not have thought about it or may see it as an area that is largely out of your control, that is simply not the case. You have the ability to create the practice you want, which includes having a team of employees that will work toward helping you reach your goals. If there are problems with your employees, it is time to take action and remedy them. Identifying problems and doing nothing about them is not going to help you have a successful practice.

There are a variety of ways you can help to improve the employees in your practice. Many practices have employees who are not engaged or who do not know their job duties as well as they should. For the latter part, give your employees the training they need in order to do their job satisfactorily. You can't expect them to perform well if they don't understand what their duties are, your company mission, or how to actually do their duties. The investment you make in training your employees is one that will provide a good return on investment.

Gallup conducted research that showed only around 30 percent of those working in the country are actually engaged in their job. Having employees who are not engaged will keep your practice from reaching its full potential. Research demonstrates that engaged employees have more initiative, are more creative, and will go above and beyond for the company they work for. That's the kind of employees you want. Problem is, you can spot the ones a mile away that don't fit the bill.

Employees who are not engaged go through the motions of their job, not really into it at all, but just getting through the day. There is no interest, no heart, and no care of whether or not they are doing their job to the best of their ability. For this type of employee, you have to take action and make a decision. You need to either replace the person, or motivate them to become engaged. It's your decision which route to take, but if you like the person and feel they have potential, there are things you can do to help engage employees, including:

- Focus on team building. When you have an office that works together as a team, each employee will be more likely to want to contribute their fair share.
- Give recognition when it is due. Oftentimes, employers are quick to point out where employees are doing things wrong or need improvement, but they overlook giving recognition when things are done right or great. Giving recognition is one of the most effective ways to get your employees motivated.
- Make sure that each of your employees is in the right position for them. For example, it makes no sense to have someone who loves paperwork and hates the phone to be the receptionist. They will be in a position where they are unlikely to give it all they got, because it is not a good fit from the start. You want each person in a position that is right for them and their strengths.
- Speak with employees so that they know what you expect from them. Whether you hold a group or individual meeting, it is important that you speak with your employees periodically. Let them know what your goals are for the practice, both short and long term, and what you expect out of employees. Most employees worth their weight will rise to the occasion.

Once you have taken the time to implement the above options, your employees should become more engaged. When your employees are engaged, you will have more success overall and will be more effective at reaching the goals you have set for your practice. Periodically review how your employees are doing. Even with doing things to engage them, you may find you have one who you just can't motivate, which may mean it is time to find a replacement that is ready to get into the game.

"I'm not the smartest fellow in the world, but I can sure pick smart colleagues."– Franklin D. Roosevelt

TURN THE PAGE

Beyond your employee engagement, there are other issues that you should put on your radar. These include such things as what you are reading, how often you are reading, how you dress, and even how you talk. Believe it or not, all of this matters. All of it is going to contribute to your success, or lack thereof. Spend time reading books that are going to help you. Now, that doesn't mean you can't have any fun and have to stick only to straight-laced business books. There are plenty of other books outside of the business genre that can teach you valuable life lessons. Seek them out, read them, and put the information into action. Even if you only get one or two nuggets of valuable information from each book, it will be well worth the time invested in reading it.

You have probably heard people talk about dressing for success. It's true – how you dress, believe it or not, makes a difference. This is because it impacts how people see you, as well as how you feel. Take a quick test to see exactly what I mean. Throw on an outfit of sweat pants and a tank top. See how you feel and how you begin acting. Perhaps you loosen up some, your speech becomes more relaxed, and you even stand and sit differently. Now try putting on a professional business outfit. Notice the difference? Immediately you act the part and begin talking, walking, and carrying yourself in a more professional manner than you did in the sweat pants. You notice it, and your patients do, too! Put forth a professional image and you will feel good, look good, and be ready to do business.

"You cannot climb the ladder of success dressed in the costume of failure."
– Zig Ziglar

TAKING MASTERMIND ACTION

I've observed doctors in practice who have been wildly successful just based on a few key concepts that they have established as cores in their practices. It's not difficult, but the truth is that you are unlikely to stumble upon truths on your own, or it is quite likely that it would take you decades before it happened. If you are lucky enough to stumble into success, great, but that route is a gamble. Taking action to reach success is not. By taking action to reach success, you will meet your goals and have the practice that you want and that you need.

In the prior chapter, mastermind groups were discussed. I can personally attest to the validity of them and how they can help your practice grow. You may be thinking about how you can reach success without having to do all of these things mentioned. My personal experience with mastermind groups, however, has been that we achieve solutions to problems that would never have materialized with just two doctors meeting or talking over the phone. Taking these measures will help ensure your success.

The bottom line when it comes to mastermind groups is that they can help you become more successful and in a shorter amount of time. You need a mentor, you need a support group. You cannot make massive progress alone. Don't think that you're alone. You are actually in good company by getting in on a mastermind group. Case in point: John D. Rockefeller, who insisted upon having daily lunches with his top advisors and leaders in his business. He did this so he could constantly and continually stimulate his mind and the "third mind" of a group in order to achieve greater and greater solutions to increasingly tougher problems as his companies grew.

Rockefeller, who was an accounting clerk, is arguably considered to be one of the wealthiest people who ever lived. He invested $4,000 in the oil refinery field and went on to earn billions. But he didn't do it alone; he surrounded himself with a team of people who could guide, advise, and keep him headed in the right direction. He had an amazing mastermind team. Adjusted for inflation, some estimate that his net worth was around $340 billion, which would make him the richest American to ever have lived.

No matter which field you look at, whether it's oil or basketball, successful people are surrounded by a mastermind group. Being able to pick their brain, bounce ideas off of them, and absorb their successful attitude is essential in helping you with your own success. Choose your friends wisely, choose your colleagues wisely, and don't overlook the importance of having your employees engaged. When you take measures to do all three of these things, success is inevitable. When you surround yourself with successful people and you become the average of the three, you will have success.

> *"A friendship founded on business is better than a business founded on friendship." – John D. Rockefeller*

[18]

Take Action to (At Least) Double Your Paycheck

DAN S. KENNEDY

WHAT YOU ARE about to read, I wrote for the very first edition of this book, in 2005. I have left it unchanged. It is even truer, more relevant, and more urgently in need of broad understanding today than then.

Here is the truth no politician, few economists, and few teachers want to tell people, and that few people want to hear: certain jobs are only worth a certain, maximum number of dollars per hour, whether you've been there doing it for one year, ten years, or thirty years. Longevity does not necessarily merit more money because the individual's length of time on the job does not necessarily increase the real value of getting that job done. (Financial problems of big bureaucracies like the U.S. postal system, the airline industry, the auto industry...our inability to compete in world markets...quality problems in our educational system....have a lot to do with the pressure on employers to pay more to people purely based on length of time on a job. Demagogue union leaders and politicians perpetuating this 100% false economy for their own gains have done irreparable harm to this country. Academics who wish to ignore how the economy really works and *must* really work have aided and abetted the fraud committed on the American public; on workers; on students being prepared for careers. The reason France has suffered with a 20% unemployment rate – yikes! – for over a decade is this foolish notion that jobs increase in value.)

As our economy is forced to acknowledge this uncomfortable reality in the years to come, there will be a great many bitter casualties.

However, hidden inside this uncomfortable truth is the secret to increasing your income literally at will.

In his book, *Earl Nightingale's Greatest Discoveries*, Earl noted that "every field of human endeavor has its stars; all the rest in these fields are in a descending order of what we might call 'the service-reward continuum.'" He went on to point out that the reason some people earn more money than others is that they have made themselves more valuable. He observed that, for the most part, the size of a person's paycheck is determined by this question – how difficult is he or she to replace?

As I was writing this, I was listening to a roundtable debate on a Sunday morning news program about employment and productivity and security in America, and a young employee had this question for management and for unions – "How will you help me avoid losing my job in the future?" Well, you see, that's the wrong question. The unions try hard to protect their turf by answering it and, as a result, they tell a big lie. Management tries hard to answer it and, as a result, they lie. Government even sticks its nose in and tries to answer it and lies. The only real truthful response is to refuse to answer it at all. What this young man needs to do is go find a full-length mirror, sit down in a chair facing it, stare deeply into his own eyes, and ask himself: "What am I going to do to avoid losing my job in the future?" The key words are "what am I going to do?" – that is the question.

And here are the extension questions:

1. What am I going to do to increase my value in the marketplace?
2. What am I going to do to demonstrably increase my value to my current employer (or clients, customers, patients)?
3. What am I going to do to increase my value to prospective future employers?
4. What am I going to do to make myself so valuable that I'm the least likely to be cut, the last to be cut?

Unfortunately, the most common responses are: "I don't have time"...."I can't afford to"..... "my employer should".... "the government should"....."Take evening classes and spend my own money? Hey, I already work hard all day. When I come home, I'm tired. And I can't afford to take classes. Besides, if these classes are going to give me skills I'll use on the job, my darned employer oughta pay for them. And I ought to get to take the classes during regular work hours. If I have to go to classes on my time, I should get time-and-a-half." Eric Hoffer wrote, "There are many who find a good alibi far more attractive than achievement."

I have sometimes been introduced, as a speaker, as The Professor of Harsh Reality. Well, here is the harsh reality every adult should come to grips with as quickly as possible, and every young person should be taught: one year, three years, and five years from now, the particular job (task) you do will not have appreciably increased in value. *You* will either have stayed the same in value or increased in value through your own initiative; that's the only way. If you have not increased in value and your job has not inherently increased in value, at some point, your employer can't or clientele won't pay more – regardless of inflation. It is at that point that your economic status shifts into reverse. Your income stagnates or declines. The gradual decline in your buying power as a consumer will prevent you from saving, investing, and creating financial security or erode what you have already accumulated. And your vulnerability to lay-off, termination or replacement increases.

This is true of the self-employed, the business owner as well. If you are not increasing your value to your customers, if you are not making yourself indispensable to them all over again, every day, then you are declining in value to them. You are either increasing in value or declining in value.

How many people do you think have this "add value" idea straight in their minds? Well, look around. One out of every ten adult Americans is on food stamps. 95% of the people reaching retirement age lack the financial resources to take care of their basic needs without all sorts of direct and disguised welfare. In most big companies, there are masses of people doing the very same jobs, the very same way year after year, even decade after decade, shocked when cheaper foreign labor or automation or some other replacement boots them out on the street. Small business owners suddenly find themselves vulnerable when a major, mass retailer or chain or aggressive new competitor comes to town. How can these terrible things happen to "good people" in America?

Every one of these people has one very distinctive thing in common; from one year to the next, they have not taken any initiative, not done anything, not invested any money or time in increasing their own personal value. *You* need to look very closely at all these folks and avoid following their example at any and all cost. And if you really would like to double your paycheck, simply take action to triple your value; one of three things will absolutely, certainly happen: 1) your present employer will respond with raises, bonuses and advancement; 2) a new employer will find and grab you; or 3) you'll discover some entrepreneurial opportunity and move on to writing your own paycheck. And if you already own a business and would like to double your paycheck, simply take action to triple your value to your customers. Your compensation will always catch up to your value.

19

Take Action to Create More Value in the Universe

DUSTIN S. BURLESON

THERE ARE MILLIONS of businesses around the country. It would be difficult to find one that is so unique that it has no competition and no other business like it. If that were the case, it would likely be fairly easy for that business to get customers. After all, it would be the only option available for those who are interested in whatever it is that they are selling. But, unfortunately, things are not that simple. We live in a country where businesses are abundant and if you are like most others in the dental field you can name several competitors within seconds.

The key, then, is differentiating yourself from your competitors. How do you do that? There are several ways, but you start with marketing. As discussed in the prior chapter, it is important that you are promoting your business. If you don't, how can you expect people to know you exist or why they should choose you over the other orthodontist down the road? It is essential that you become the marketer of your business and the visionary of your company, not just someone that is doing the work once people are in the chair.

Along the way to becoming the doctor you are today you learned all about treating patients, but there is a good chance you didn't learn a lot about marketing or the process of promoting your business. Yet it is essential if you want to have a successful practice. You must remove the time to dollar equation and instead install the value to the dollar equation. In other words, you may think that marketing your business is not worth your time. Your time would be better spent working on the next patient. The value that the marketing brings to your business makes it worth the effort you are putting in. And it helps keep people in that chair so that you have someone to treat when you walk into your office each day.

"You can get everything in life you want if you will just help enough other people get what they want."– Zig Ziglar

SMILES COUNT

There are a lot of things that you can do to market your practice. We won't go into all those, as you may be familiar with some. There are some things you can do to market your business that may be costly. Without trying them, you may never even know if they are worth the return on investment. But there are some things you can do that are small, simple, and yet pay off with big results.

For starters, you want to provide your employees with the training that they need to continue adding value and experience to your office. Watch for things that are low or no cost, yet will improve the experience that people have when they step into your office. Some of the things you can do to help with this are to greet your patients by their name, give them a fond farewell, write handwritten thank-you cards, follow-up with phone calls, be on time with the appointments, and make social notes to build relationships with your clients, customers, and patients.

The personal touch you provide is going to go a lot farther than you ever realize. This goes for outside of the office as well. If you happen to see one of your patients outside of the office, it goes without saying that you should be friendly with them and acknowledge them, even if you can't recall their name. One woman I know shared with me about how she took her kids to a pediatrician on several occasions who was decent during office visit, but he could have been friendlier. What prompted her to find a new doctor's office was when she twice, kids in tow, saw the doctor outside of the office in a local store. She said hello to him twice, reminding him that he was the children's doctor. He gave her the cold shoulder both times, acting as if it were a bother to merely smile and say hello to her outside of the office.

Little does that doctor know that when it happened the first time she assumed he was busy or had his mind occupied, but when it happened a second time, mom began looking for a new doctor. Who wants to go to a doctor who can't even be courteous enough to be friendly and say hello when seeing you in the store? Months later, she encountered a similar public encounter with her new doctor, and she wanted to test it to see what the woman would be like. She was pleased that when she said hello to the doctor the woman stopped, was friendly, and asked how the children were doing. At that moment, mom's decision to switch doctors was confirmed as being the right one.

"A warm smile is the universal language of kindness."
– William Arthur Ward

PERSONAL TOUCH

Small gestures go a long way toward creating a personal touch and experience for your patients. A smile, whether inside the office or when you see a patient of yours at the grocery store, costs nothing. Yet it says a lot about you and helps to form how others see you as a doctor.

You never know what is going to resonate with someone. I had a patient who kept one of my personal notes of encouragement for years and actually had stuck it to his wardrobe mirror in college to remind him that he could achieve great things. The words of encouragement that I wrote to that patient, and the ones you write to your patients, can help to change a life. It can also change your paycheck, although that should not be the reason that you do it. That patient of mine had referred no less than $100,000 of additional business to my practice. For the cost of a stamp and an encouraging word, the business earned was over $100,000.

WHAT YOU GET BACK

Good things come to those who give. You have heard that and other sayings along those lines before. But have you ever thought about it and put it into action? What we get is usually a reflection of what it is that we are giving to the world. If you give kindness, you will get kindness in return. Being an orthodontist, that kindness may come in the form of patient referrals and increased business. Don't just be what you do, be a marketer and promoter of your practice. Smile, the smiles will come back to you in more ways than one.

As an orthodontist, you know the value of a smile. You create amazing smiles for a living. But you may not realize how important they are psychologically. A smile is so powerful to improving one's mood and how one feels that you can trick your mind into being happy. This has been scientifically proven by researchers who study the psychology of the smile. The next time you are feeling down, just put a smile on your face for a few minutes. Just sit and smile. When you make yourself smile, even if you are not happy, you are using the zygomatic major muscles, which control the corners of your mouth. When you use those, it makes your brain think that you have something to be happy about, and it purposely begins making you feel happy. So the next time you feel rushed or stressed, literally put on a smile before meeting with your next patient. Putting the smile on first will create a happy brain and help to turn your day around!

Take stock in the small ways you can create a bond with your patients and give them a better experience. When they have a favorable opinion of you and your practice, they are going to help do a lot of the promoting for you. Word of mouth advertising is the most powerful form of promoting your business that there is. By and large, people trust word of mouth referrals far more than they do any outright advertising that you can do. Create happy patients and you will without a doubt have more patients sent your way.

20

Take Action to Promote Yourself, Your Ideas, Your Business, Products, and Services

Dan S. Kennedy

SOME YEARS BACK, I had lunch with Coach Bill Foster, then in charge of the entire Southwest Conference of college basketball, after a long, incredibly distinguished coaching career. Bill gave the famous Jim Valvano his first coaching job. Bill had a phenomenal tenure at Duke and then at the University of South Carolina. *Esquire* featured him as "Dale Carnegie on the basketball court," because of his reputation as a powerful motivator. He turned Northwestern's program around. In every case, everywhere Bill went, attendance soared, alumni support increased, and community involvement with the team improved dramatically. Bottom-line: Bill Foster knows how to fill seats.

And that's what we talked about at lunch; what he was busily doing for the SWC's schools, most with sagging attendance; teaching and motivating coaches to become promoters, and relentlessly promoting. The year before Bill, the tournament's big Tip-Off Luncheon, for example, had only 300 in attendance; Bill's first year, 1,000; and Bill's goal for the next one, 1,500 – a 500% increase in two seasons. Schools with game attendance down to 2,000 will, with a single season, climb to 4,500 with Bill's determined influence.

What Bill Foster Knows About Success That Most People Don't (Or Don't Want To)

Here's what Bill told me, that everybody needs to hear and take to heart (whether they like it or not): Coaches, he told me, often don't understand that what they do off the basketball court, all year round, in their communities and with the national media, promoting, is as important as what they do on the court – because, if attendance sags, the university's easiest fix is to fire the coach and bring in a new coach, with new excitement and new promises. Because, if attendance sags, recruiting suffers. Because, if attendance sags, player confidence and commitment suffer.

In other words, a very, very important part of the coach's responsibility is promotion. In other words, the "core" of coaching (like the "core" of operating a restaurant, owning a pet shop, writing books, being a jeweler, whatever) is not of sole importance; it is not the key to success. The smart coach is an assertive, creative promoter. "One of the signs on my wall says, a terrible thing happens when you don't promote," Bill said, smiling. "Nothing."

I have watched Bill's career closely, and I'll tell you something; if you didn't know where he was, you could figure it out just by collecting and looking at the promotional literature, the calendars, the newsletters, the mailings of each school. One would stand out above all others. And that's where you'd find Bill Foster.

You see, in *every* field of endeavor, in *any* field of endeavor, the winners are promoters.

Now, some people will want to argue about how unfair that is. I saw some clown from the American Bar Association on a talk show the other day blaming the legal profession's disfavor with the public on "those attorneys who do a lot of advertising." At Arizona State University, the academic in-crowd just about ostracized the professor who turned *Where There's A Will, There's An 'A'* into a giant nationwide bestseller, making himself famous and rich along the way. That's all crap. It's jealousy. Ego speaking. Those unwilling to promote are always the biggest, most vocal critics of those successful through promotion. Pick any field and you'll find both. You'll find very vocal critics of promoters. And you'll find tremendously successful promoters.

General Patton was viewed by many of his peers as a shameless, egotistical promoter. Madonna, throughout her career, has been sneered at as a no-talent self-promoter. Countless, ultimately respected and celebrated leaders in every imaginable field have risen to the mountaintop or brought themselves back from failure and disgrace via relentless, widely criticized self-promotion. And let's add the adage, "There have been many statues erected to honor those highly criticized, but very few statues erected to critics."

You Only Get To Choose From Door #1 or Door #2

You really have two choices. You can choose to stick your nose up at the promoters, criticize them and criticize promotion, view it as unseemly, as beneath you, as crass, and stand around grumbling about it. Or you can get good at it and use it to create influence, prominence, prestige, credibility, celebrity, career and financial success. It is your choice.

The coaches Bill works with face these choices. Some of those who choose "Door #1" will lose their current positions and move down to smaller schools, and there they may very well find happiness, peace of mind, a "home", and that's okay. Many, though, will move down and be puzzled and embittered by it. They'll live forever in envy of others they judge to be less qualified, less capable coaches than they are. The world is full of such people.

A few will pick "Door #2". They'll get the message. They'll somehow get intellectually and emotionally okay with the way things really are. They'll dig in and learn and adapt and grow. They'll become great promoters. And those are the coaches whose names you and I will know.

Let me now try and summarize the message.

Waiting around to be discovered, to be recognized, to be noticed, to be appointed, to be promoted guarantees one thing and one thing only: old age. Focusing on doing whatever it is that you do better than anybody else and trusting that that alone is enough (and arguing tirelessly that it should be enough) guarantees one thing and one thing only: a long life of labor in oblivion.

If Jesus had hung around his hometown working as a carpenter, giving his talks at the local Kiwanis Club meeting, writing books that never got published, waiting to be discovered, we might all be Zen Buddhists today. He was a pretty bold, bombastic promoter. Turned wet bread into fish. Healed the blind. Pitched a fit about the merchants hanging around the temple. Well, you know the story. I don't have to tell you about it. You know the story because Jesus was such a great promoter.

21

Take Action to Eliminate the Competition

DUSTIN S. BURLESON

TAKE A MOMENT and consider what your education or training was regarding marketing up to this point. As you were going through dental school and orthodontic residency, you had many classes, studied a great deal, and learned so much information about how to help people. But what did you learn about getting the word of your services out to those people to get them in your door in the first place?

If you are like most of us in this field, you didn't learn anything, and what little was discussed left us feeling that marketing is either a bad thing or it is completely unnecessary. Neither of which is true, and believing in both will keep you from ever attaining the goals you have for your practice. As doctors, we are taught this negative association with marketing either through direct or indirect routes, but we walk away with the same beliefs all the same. Now is the time to change them.

CHANGING LIVES

If you believe, as I do, that what we do for a living changes the lives of patients, that it improves their lives, then don't we have an obligation to let them know about it? Sure we do! We are passionate about what we do because we know the difference it makes in someone's life. There is nothing like a great smile or seeing someone go from hiding their smile to showing it off with pleasure. A great smile gives people a level of confidence that may be difficult to gain elsewhere.

You have the ability to give people this life-changing smile. As such, you have a moral obligation to tell as many people as you can about your service or product. Something so great for the masses should not be hidden. Everyone should know that the service is available and what it can do for them. And I mean what it can do for them beyond just the great smile. I mean the way the end results of a successful treatment can be life-changing. People need to know that you can do that for them, and they will learn about it through your marketing efforts.

"With confidence, you have won before you have started." – Zig Ziglar

THE COMPETITION

When you begin to do some marketing, you may take some flack from your friends, family, and especially from your competition. They will not be happy about the fact that you are promoting your services. It's odd to think that anyone beyond your competition will care that you are marketing your business, but you will be surprised at how it strikes a nerve with so many people. Always keep in mind that it is seeded in jealousy. They have the same opportunity to build their business and to promote their ideas and services. They choose to not do so, but they will be annoyed that you have. You are a reminder to them of all they could be doing and are choosing not to.

If you want to have a successful practice, you have to overlook and ignore what others think about you marketing your business. It's just that straightforward. You pay too much attention to what they think and start listening to it by choosing to not market your practice, and you will need to ask which ones among them are willing to help pay your bills and increase your salary.

There was a point in my career when I seriously considered ending all of the principles that I have laid out in this book. It was the day I received a letter from an angry orthodontist in my town who was severely displeased to learn that we were advertising via direct mail, magazine, radio, etc. I was so concerned with getting other people to like me that I let the one person in my town affect me who will never pay me a penny.

There is only one other person in your town who will never use your service and never pay you a penny. That person will never give your kids a hug when they come home and never help you pay for their college. Nor will that person put food on the table for them, and that, for you, is your competitor.

When I got serious about producing results and acknowledged that I would have some enemies in the process, the practice began to grow exponentially. Competition is healthy. It provides better services at the best cost possible for the consumer. Don't shy away from it and don't let your competitors make you feel bad for doing something so obviously successful that they could be doing the same thing and getting the same result. Don't worry, either, as many of the competitors in your area will write your success off as "luck" or some other "unattainable quality" that they could never achieve, like an ideal location, affiliation, history of success in your family, or something as trivial as your youth or old age, good looks, or gender. Your competitors will say things like "well, if I was X, Y, and Z, then I could do the same thing."

Jealousy is a horrible human character trait, and you should stay as far away from it as possible.

> *"The thermometer of success is merely the jealousy of the malcontents."*
> *– Salvador Dali*

STAYING FOCUSED

I don't want to scare you and make you think that you are going to get this massive backlash for putting your name out there. But I want to prepare you. Putting your name out there makes you a big target for those who have nothing better to do than throw darts. But don't fold under the pressure. If it is bringing patients in the door, you are doing the right thing. If it is helping to take care of your family and the families of those who work for you, then you are doing the right thing.

Worry about you and only you. Forget about what anyone else thinks about what you are doing. In life, you have to stay focused on you, your success and goals, and looking forward. If you spend your time looking back at those who you are competing with, you will slow yourself down, get tripped up, and will not be as successful as you could. Keep looking forward, doing things to reach your goals, and focusing on your own success. You will get there faster than you ever thought possible.

22

It's Not Enough to Act on Your Ideas – The Only Reliable Path to Maximum Success is Maximum Action

DAN S. KENNEDY

MY SPEAKING COLLEAGUE Jim Rohn says that when you look closely at the highly successful individual in any field, you walk away saying to yourself: "It's no wonder he's doing so well...look at everything he's doing."

Well, there's a darned good test! If we followed you around for a week and painstakingly recorded how you spent your time, what you did every day to advance your career or business, would we wind up saying to ourselves "It's no wonder he's doing so well – look at everything he's doing"?

The truth is that most people are intellectually lazy, surprisingly uncurious in their acquisition of information. And, in their businesses, they lazily rely on only one, two or three methods of attracting customers or clients. As a consultant, quite frankly, I do not walk away from most clients saying "It's no wonder he's doing so well; look at everything he's doing." Mostly, I say to myself: "It's a miracle he's doing as well as he is – look at how little he's doing."

I once knew a chiropractor who built three million dollar a year practices. Not one, three. Dr. S. built and sold one, moved to another community, built and sold another one, and one's a fluke but three's a system, so the word spread and a whole lot of doctors wanted to know how he did that. So many, so much, so that thousands each paid $30,000.00 to come and hear him expound on his methods in seminars. But the essence of his success was really quite simple. Invariably, every doctor asked him the same question: "How can I get __ new patients this month?" How can I get 30 new patients this month? How can I get 50 new patients this month? The number varied, but the question was always the same. And so was Dr. S.'s answer: "I don't know one way to get 30 new patients, but I know 30 ways to get a new patient, and I use every single one of them."

See, if you need new clients for your business, don't do one thing, do a dozen things. If you have a problem to solve, don't implement one possible solution; implement a dozen. One of the speakers I appeared with frequently was Reverend Robert Schuller, and he's become famous for his story of how he faced the massive cost overruns in completing The Crystal Cathedral. Confronted with a need for ten million dollars, he made a list of ten different ways he might raise that money. Then he went to work on all ten simultaneously.

In my Renegade Millionaire System, I focus in depth and at length bordering on the tedious, on this important point of counter-intuitive differentiation between highly successful people and the majority. Everyone was taught and conditioned to do things sequentially, step by step, one thing at a time, in as orderly and organized and logical a way as possible. The majority stick with this, the exceptionally successful – at some point – dump it by the roadside and, instead, engage in the barely controlled chaos of simultaneous initiatives, remedies and actions. They cook up success in very messy kitchens.

Take action to diversify the way that money and success comes to you, the way that you solve problems, even the way that you acquire new information and grow as a person.

Curiosity, incidentally, is a wonderful thing. Forget the old "curiosity killed the cat" thing; curiosity is what uncovers opportunities and makes people rich. The average child of 5 to 10 asks hundreds of questions a day; the average adult asks only a handful. This is why kids have so much energy and enthusiasm for living. This is also why adults age prematurely and rapidly. Life-force itself comes from curiosity and creativity. "Always Be Creating and Discovering, with Enthusiasm." When it becomes "went there, did that", you have at least one foot in the grave.

WHAT KIND OF ACTION YIELDS THE GREATEST RESULTS?

Yes, there is one type or kind of action that produces maximum results in a minimum length of time, thanks in part to the principle of momentum. Again, it's from Jim Rohn that I first heard about the incredibly powerful Principle of Massive Action. The key word here is: Massive.

Not tiny action. Not wimpy action. Not tentative action. Not toe-in-the-water action. Not ponderously slow action. Massive action.

In 1946, a man named Walter Russell had his philosophies published, largely because he was such an unusual, larger-than-life figure. Russell never went past elementary school, and his first job was a clerk in a dry goods store earning $2.50 a week. To the amazement of just about everybody who knew of his "non-background," Russell achieved considerable fame and success as an architect, sculptor, and artist. With the publication of his success philosophies, Russell became known as "the man who tapped the secrets of the universe." Russell insisted that every man has consummate genius within, and taught that "every successful man or genius has three particular qualities in common, and the most conspicuous of these is that they all produce a prodigious amount of work."

In his classic *Lead The Field* recordings, Earl Nightingale told, with slight sarcasm, of the man who arrives home everyday and says to his family, "Boy am I tired" – because that's what he heard his father say every day when he arrived home from work at a job under conditions that really warranted the expression of exhaustion. I am often impressed at how little work people are willing to do in order to get what they insist they want.

Let me give you an example of the Principle of Massive Action in action: a woman, Barbara L., cornered me at a seminar, introduced herself as the CEO of a specialized, industrial company – in her words, a woman in a man's world, and told me of her frustrations and woes with finding financing. She was literally turning away lucrative manufacturing contracts because she couldn't finance the necessary raw materials, labor, and other costs while in production and then waiting to be paid a month or so following delivery. Having once run a specialty manufacturing company with similar problems, I instantly had empathy – and ideas – for her, but first I asked some questions. And I was not surprised to discover that she had tried most local banks, suffered rejection, and pretty much given up.

From my own experience, I knew Barbara had stopped at only scratching the surface of potential solutions. But she was no different than most. Most people, confronted with a problem, think of and try only a few solutions, and give up quite easily. This, incidentally, is the blunt truth behind many of our popularized societal ills and failures. Most people who "can't" get jobs actually have given up on getting a job. People who "can't" get off welfare have truthfully given up getting off of welfare. Here's why this is inarguably true: because there are people just like them who have persevered and gotten jobs, who have persevered and gotten off welfare. If one can, everyone can.

So, just as example, here was my prescription for Barbara:

1. Strengthen the proposal package and re-contact every bank that said no. Then keep re-contacting them and bringing them up-to-date every thirty days.

2. Reach out to friends, associates, community contacts, vendors in search of recommendations of other lenders and/or somebody who has a relationship of some kind with someone of authority in one of those banks.

3. Discuss different formats for the financing: revolving receivables credit line or asset-based long term loan or 90-day notes. Ask the banks for different things.

4. Contact banks outside the local market...draw a 300-mile circle around the plant and contact every bank in that circle.

5. Consider a sale/leaseback arrangement with a leasing company for all the equipment and furniture in the factory and offices.

6. Contact the SBA. Through the SBA, get put in touch with SBA Certified Lenders. And investigate the SBA's preferred lending services for women-owned businesses.

7. Get free help through the SBA, from SCORE (Service Corps Of Retired Executives) for beefing up the business plan, proposal, etc.

8. Meet with key vendors and discuss creative, extended terms that could equate to the same effect as a loan or credit line. Simultaneously, open up conversations with new, alternative vendors who might use credit as a means of acquiring new business.

9. Consider factoring some receivables. Meet with factoring companies and brokers.

10. Offer customers a significant discount for paying 50% to 100% of the contracts in advance. (There is a cost of financing, no matter how you do it. You can convert that cost to a discount for prepayment without impact on true, net profit.)

11. Advertise for private lenders and "angels."

12. Form a new limited partnership or corporation with private investors, which will serve as a financing-for-profit business, lending against your other company's receivables.

13. Franchise or pseudo-franchise exclusive sales territories, and use the fees collected from that to establish your own financing fund.

14. Alter the nature of your business, the "mix" of your business, so you can get some cash-with-order business.

15. Through blind, confidential advertising, put the entire business up for sale and test the waters.

16. Meet with key employees and discuss possibilities for assembling receivables financing or equity investment from employees.

Now, here's the "trick" I shared with Barbara: do all 16 of these things at the same time. Right now. Fast. Back when I ran a company with its nose pushed up against this same wall, I did all 16 of these things. In our case, we succeeded with numbers 3, 5, 8, 10 and 14. #10 alone, incidentally, dramatically altered the company's cash flow situation, even though everybody told me that the clients in our industry would never pre-pay for their manufacturing orders. In three months, we converted over half the existent clients to pre-paying, for a 10% discount.

But if we had tried one, done everything we could before giving up on one, *then* tried two, done everything we could with two, *then* tried three....it's pretty obvious that time's going to win and we're going to lose.

Of course, she might have responded – as most would – with "Geez, that's a lot of work!" And she might have said, "How am I supposed to get all that done?" ...and... "But I don't know how to do all those things?".... or "I'll be working until midnight everyday to do all that." Etc. But I'm delighted to report that Barbara found an SBA Certified Lender bank, secured a long-term loan replacing all her other financing and providing expansion capital, and she found three private individuals happy to finance individual, large receivables from new contracts as she needs them. And it's no wonder Barbara finally got her financing; look at everything she did!

COULD YOU CULTIVATE THE MOST PRIZED PERSONAL CHARACTERISTIC OF ANY AND ALL KNOWN TO MAN?

Let me give you one other example, which leads us to yet another important success behavior: in Fort Wayne, Indiana, for me, disaster struck; the set-up crew for the seminar tour called me in my hotel room the afternoon before the event to tell me that none of my product was at the convention center. Everyone at my office's end then did everything they thought they could do to correct the problem, to get UPS to deliver early the next day, to try and trace the location of the shipment. They did everything they thought they could do, but they still stopped short of doing everything that could be done. As concerned and earnest as they were, they stopped short. Why? Because very, very few people understand the idea of refusing to accept anything less than success.

After they gave up, I dug in. Through a series of phone calls and conversations, I finally got the guy standing on the right receiving dock, in Ft. Wayne, Indiana. I sold him – and I mean: sold – on getting up early the next morning, getting to his warehouse, and going through the carloads of boxes left there during the night to find mine. And to call me by 7:00 AM that morning with the good news that he had done so. And, a little after 7:00 AM, he was on the phone. And he had the boxes loaded in his own, personal pick-up truck. And he brought them to the convention center, undoubtedly in violation of a handful of company regulations. And, for you cynics, I didn't offer him money, he never asked for money, and when we finally tried to give him money that morning, he refused it. Now, I honestly believe that I did not do anything here that anybody else couldn't have done. This was not a matter of "talent." I just refused to accept anything less than success. I stayed at it long enough and hard enough that I got a little "earned luck", and found a guy like me – two people who can and will "carry the message to Garcia." If you don't know the story of the man who carried the message to Garcia, I've reprinted it here. It reveals the most prized characteristic on earth.

A Message to Garcia

In all this Cuban business there is one man stands out on the horizon of my memory like Mars at perihelion.

When war broke out between Spain and the United States, it was very necessary to communicate quickly with the leader of the Insurgents. Garcia was somewhere in the mountain vastness of Cuba – no one knew where. The President must secure his cooperation, and quickly.

What to do!

Someone said to the President, "There is a fellow by the name of Rowan will find Garcia for you, if anybody can."

Rowan was sent for and given a letter to be delivered to Garcia. How the "fellow by the name of Rowan" took the letter, sealed it up in an oilskin pouch, strapped it over his heart, in four days landed by night off the cost of Cuba from an open boat, disappeared on the other side of the Island, having traversed a hostile country on foot, and delivered his letter to Garcia – are things I have no special desire now to tell in detail. The point that I wish to make is this: McKinley gave Rowan a letter to be delivered to Garcia; Rowan took the letter and did not ask, "Where is he at?"

By the Eternal! there is a man whose form should be cast in deathless bronze and the statue placed in every college of the land. It is not book-learning young men need, nor instruction about this and that, but a stiffening of the vertebrae which will cause them to be loyal to a trust, to act promptly, concentrate their energies: do the thing "Carry a message to Garcia."

General Garcia is dead now, but there are other Garcias. No man who has endeavored to carry out an enterprise where many hands were needed, but has been well-nigh appalled at times by the imbecility of the average man – the inability or unwillingness to concentrate on a thing and do it.

Slipshod assistance, foolish inattention, dowdy indifference, and half-hearted work seem the rule; and no man succeeds, unless by hook or crook or threat he forced or bribes other men to assist him; or mayhap, God in His goodness performs a miracle, and sends him an Angel of Light for an assistant.

You, reader, put this matter to a test: You are sitting now in your office – six clerks are within call. Summon any one and make this request: "Please look in the encyclopedia and make a brief memorandum for me concerning the life of Correggio."

Will the clerk quietly say, "Yes, sir," and go do the task?

On your life he will not. He will look at you out of a fishy eye and ask one or more of the following questions:

Who was he?

Which encyclopedia?

Where is the encyclopedia?

Was I hired for that?

Don't you mean Bismarck?

What's the matter with Charlie doing it?

Is he dead?

Is there any hurry?

Shan't I bring you the book and let you look it up yourself?

What do you want to know for?

And I will lay you ten to one that after you have answered the questions, and explained how to find the information, and why you want it, the clerk will go off and get one of the other clerks to help him try to find Garcia – and then come back and tell you there is no such man. Of course I may lose my bet, but according to the Law Of Average I will not.

Now, if you are wise, you will not bother to explain to your "assistant" that Correggio is indexed under the C's, not in the K's, but you will smile very sweetly and say, "Never mind," and go look it up yourself. And this incapacity for independent action, this moral stupidity, this infirmity of the will, this unwillingness to cheerfully catch hold and lift – these are the things that put pure Socialism so far into the future. If men will not act for themselves, what will they do when the benefit of their effort is for all?

A fist mate with knotted club seems necessary; and the dread of getting "the bounce" Saturday night holds many a worker to his place. Advertise for a stenographer, and nine out of ten who apply can neither spell nor punctuate – and do not think it necessary to.

Can such a one write a letter to Garcia?

"You see that bookkeeper," said the foreman to me in a large factory.

"Yes; what about him?"

"Well, he's a fine accountant, but if I'd send him up town on an errand, he might accomplish the errand all right, and on the other hand, might stop at four saloons on the way, and when he got to Main Street would forget what he had been sent for."

Can such a man be entrusted to carry a message to Garcia?

We have recently been hearing much maudlin sympathy expressed for the "downtrodden denizens of the sweatshop" and the "homeless wanderer searching for honest employment," and with it all often go many hard words for the men in power.

Nothing is said about the employer who grows old before his time in a vain attempt to get frowzy ne'er-do-wells to do intelligent work; and his long, patient striving after "help" that does nothing but loaf when his back is turned. In every store and factory there is a constant weeding-out process going on. The employer is constantly sending away "help" that have shown their incapacity to further the interests of the business, and others are being taken on. No matter how good times are, this sorting continues: only, if times are hard and work is scarce, the sorting is done finer – but out and forever out the incompetent and unworthy go. It is the survival of the fittest. Self-interest prompts every employer to keep the best – those who can carry a message to Garcia.

I know one man of really brilliant parts who has not the ability to manage a business of his own, and yet who is absolutely worthless to anyone else, because he carries with him constantly the insane suspicion that his employer is oppressing, or intending to oppress, him. He cannot give orders, and he will not receive them. Should a message be given him, to take to Garcia, his answer would probably be, "Take it yourself!"

Tonight this man walks the streets looking for work, the wind whistling through his threadbare coat. No one who knows him dare employ him, for he is a regular firebrand of discontent. He is impervious to reason, and the only thing that can impress him is the toe of a thick-soled Number Nine boot.

Of course, I know that one so morally deformed is no less to be pitied than a physical cripple; but in our pitying let us drop a tear, too, for the men who are striving to carry on a great enterprise, whose working hours are not limited by the whistle, and whose hair is fast turning white through the struggle to hold in line dowdy indifference, slipshod imbecility, and the heartless ingratitude which, but for their enterprise, would be both hungry and homeless.

Have I put the matter too strongly? Possibly I have; but when all the world has done a-slumming I wish to speak a word of sympathy for the man who succeeds – the man who, against great odds, has directed the efforts of others, and having succeeded, finds there's nothing in it: nothing but bare board and clothes. I have carried a dinner-pail and worked for a day's wages, and I have also been an employer of labor, and I know there is something to be said on both sides. There is no excellence, per se, in poverty; rags are no recommendation; and all employers are not rapacious and high-handed, any more than all poor men are virtuous. My heart goes out to the man who does his work when the "boss" is away, as well as when he is at home. And the man who, when given a letter for Garcia, quietly takes the missive, without asking any idiotic questions, and with no lurking intention of chucking it into the nearest sewer, or of doing naught else but deliver it, never gets "laid off," nor has to go on a strike for higher wages. Civilization is one long, anxious search for just such individuals. Anything such a man asks shall be granted. He is wanted in every city, town and village – in every office, shop, store and factory. The world cries out for such; he is needed and needed badly – the man who can "Carry a Message to Garcia."

[23]

Take Simultaneous Action on Many Fronts

Dustin S. Burleson

WHAT DO YOU think of when you consider taking action? If you are like most people I work with in coaching, you can rattle off a few things here and there, but most of them will do nothing in the way of helping to make your practice more successful. Problem is, people today are busier than ever before, but they are usually busy doing all the wrong things!

I see this with orthodontists on a regular basis. They tell me all the areas in their life where they are taking action. When they do the problem with why they are not reaching the level of success they want, it immediately becomes clear. They are spending their time doing too many meaningless things that will get them nowhere. That's not to say you should never engage in meaningless tasks. But it does mean they shouldn't be consuming much of your time. We get out of life what we put into it, and if you spend your time doing a lot of meaningless tasks, you are not bound to get much in return.

Take your to-do list, for example. Whether you have your to-do list written down or stored in your head, you likely have one. We all do and it's not a bad thing. It all comes down to what's on that to-do list. If you have the right things on it, you will be working your way toward reaching your goals. To-do lists are great for getting people to take action. But if the to-do list is filled with things like mow the lawn, pull weeds, and wash the car, there is a really good chance your time could be better spent doing something else. If you have such things on your list, it is important to realize that your time is more valuable than that. Unless you really love cutting your grass, you can probably get a neighborhood kid who will do it for a very reasonable price, and you can use that time to instead spend it with your kids, your spouse, on your business, or doing something relaxing to recharge your batteries.

"It seems essential, in relationships and all tasks, that we concentrate only on what is most significant and important." – Søren Kierkegaard

What to Do

I often have coaching clients who ask me what that one thing is that they should be doing. My response is always the same – "everything!" That is the truth and there is no way of getting around it. As discussed in the prior chapter, if you want to be successful, you will have to do a lot more than one thing. One thing will not get you to where you want to be. One thing will never make your business the successful practice you want it to be. One thing is simply not good enough. You have to do it all. You have to look for and utilize every angle and every opportunity.

Those who stop short with doing just one thing will never reach the level of success that they want. Successful people do many things in order to get where they are. Those "many things" may vary, but they are doing them all. As an orthodontist or dentist, there are many things that you should be doing in order to grow your practice and be the most successful doctor in town. We have gone over many of them in this book, but they all come down to one thing – taking action. You must take action in order to succeed.

Everyone wants to be successful. Everyone worth their weight in salt speaks to working hard and making gains in their profession, their business, and their relationships. Yet what I've noticed is that very few people actually take massive action toward identified and written-down goals and objectives. With "written-down" being the important action words that need to happen to keep you on the right track, working toward those goals.

If you don't write your goals down, they are only half-way achieved. Writing them down makes the idea real, concrete, and sets the wheels in motion to make it happen. When achieving new goals, the smartest clients in my private coaching groups write them down. Then, they share them with their spouse, close friend, and they even laminate them and post them on their bathroom mirror, the dashboard of their car, or pin them to the bulletin board above their desk at work.

The point here is that successful people are relentless in pursuing the results of their goals. If you don't have them written down and put somewhere you can be reminded of them each day, you may forget, get off track, or not take daily action toward making them happen.

"Obstacles are those frightful things you see when you take your eyes off your goal." – Henry Ford

Research suggests that some 70 percent of goals that people set on New Year's Eve are never achieved. You know how it goes. The shiny ball in New York City is about to drop and you choose the goals that you are going to achieve in the New Year. They usually involve things like losing weight, quitting smoking, or to exercise more. We all know that most of those goals don't end up being achieved, but have we ever considered why that is? There are a few reasons. First, many people are not serious about the goals when they make them. For many people, it has become a habit to rattle off that they are going to lose weight that year, that they are going to "finally do it." The other reason is that those goals are usually made in haste, are not written down, and the person does very little throughout the year in order to reach them.

In fact, places like gyms and weight loss programs bank on the fact that people will not achieve those goals. They sign up millions of people in the first week of January. They sign them to lengthy contracts. Yet they know full well that the majority of them will not be working out or dieting six months later. A few will drop off right away, a few more in the coming weeks, and by spring, most of the people who signed up are long gone and back to eating Krispy Kreme donuts, talking about how they will do it "next year."

I've seen people do this very thing in their professional lives. I've worked with people in coaching who do the same thing. Set the same goal each year, give it no thought, move on and get stuck in their routine, and then make the same goal again the following year. You can achieve your goals and have a successful practice. But it takes action, not just idle words that are spoken in haste and soon forgotten.

Do you want to know what separates your practice from the most successful one in your city or state? Action. That's it. Everything boils down to action. It's all about the action that the person leading those practices took. That's all they have on you at this point. They have simply acted and done things to make their goals a reality. There is no reason on this earth why you can't do exactly the same thing!

The Power of Positive

If there is one thing that you should have gained from this book beyond the importance of taking action, it is the power of positive thinking. There is so much power in positive thinking, and yet so few people realize it. Actually, those who are successful do realize it; it is those who don't and those who struggle that don't realize the power in it. You can set goals all day long, and even write them down and share them with others, but at the end of the day if you don't believe you can accomplish them, you are in big trouble.

You have to believe in the fact that you can achieve the goals you write down. You have to believe that you have what it takes to "Carry the Message to Garcia." If you don't, you are not going to get very far. You will become your own biggest obstacle. If you believe in yourself and your ability to overcome challenges, find solutions, and take action to achieve your goals, then there is just one thing you need to know – nothing can stop you.

Another thing that separates successful people from those that don't reach their goals, or possibly never even set any, is perseverance. Successful people don't expect that success will happen overnight. They realize that it is going to take hard work and that it is going to take time. But they know that once they stick with it that they will persevere and reach their goals and attain the level of success that they are seeking.

Number One

Being number one takes work. It takes action. Just consider Vince Lombardi. Arguably one of the best coaches, if not the best, in any type of sport throughout history. The man's record speaks for itself to demonstrate what a success he was. He had 5 NFL championships and has been inducted into various halls of fame. He knew what it took to bring out the best in his players and get them to work hard in order to achieve. He wasn't shy about letting people know what he thought it took to be number one, or what it took to succeed. And he thought this went for anything in life – football to running a business. He believed that you had to give it your all. You can't show up to the field, or the office, and give it half of what you have. You have to give it 100 percent all the time. It's just that simple.

Lombardi put it this way "Running a football team is no different than running any other kind of organization – an army, a political party, or a business. The principles are the same. The object is to win – to beat the other guy. Maybe that sounds hard or cruel. I don't think it is."

If you want to win, and I think you do, then you have to do what Lombardi believed separated the successful players from the ones that came in second place. You have to give it your all, all of the time.

24

Take Action to Turn Failure into Success

DAN S. KENNEDY

I ONCE SAW a particularly ornery dog latch onto a mailman's leg. The mailman shook his leg but the dog held on, growling menacingly. The mailman kicked the dog with his other leg. The dog held on. The mailman dragged the dog down the sidewalk. The dog held on. The mailman sprayed the dog with Mace. He hit the dog on the head with his mail sack. He swung his leg, dog attached, into a tree trunk. The dog held on. I thought to myself: there is the dog version of Dan Kennedy.

In his best-selling book, *Swim with the Sharks*, Harvey MacKay tells of being turned down by all his local lending institutions. Then he drew a 3-inch circle on the map around his city and called on all the banks within that circle. They all turned him down, too. He drew a bigger circle. Eventually he got his loan. He says he'd still be drawing ever-bigger circles if he hadn't connected. I believe him.

If you look at most highly successful entrepreneurs, you won't find markedly superior talent, intelligence, education, or resources. Self-made millionaires are surprisingly ordinary – and, often, surprisingly unintelligent – people. Conversely, a small percentage of Mensa members are self-made millionaires. So it ain't intelligence. Instead, it seems to have much to do with a profound sort of stubbornness.

How You Deal With Failure Determines Whether Or Not You Ever Get To Deal With Success

Research supervised by a professor at Tulane University revealed that the average entrepreneur goes through 3.8 failures before achieving significant success.

Actually, the entire entrepreneurial experience is one of frequent failure interrupted by occasional success. The entire experience of selling is one of frequent refusal (rejection) interrupted by occasional acceptance. In direct marketing, we call it "testing", not failure. But a whole lot more "tests" fail than succeed.

Go Ahead, Screw Up, Fall Down.

Embarrass Yourself.

A Lot. Fast.

There IS value in making mistakes. General Schwarzkopf discussed one situation he encountered where, if a bundle of decisions were made and actions taken and 49% turned out wrong, everybody'd still be way ahead of where they were with no decisions being made and no actions taken. I say: screw up. Fall down. The opposite requires living in constant fear of error, and that's a sad, pitiful existence. You have to look at every significant accomplishment as the end result of a certain number of successes but also a certain number of failures.

When I first wrote this book, Billy Crystal was one of Hollywood's hottest comic actors. His movie *City Slickers* was a huge hit, birthing a sequel. But his movie *Mr. Saturday Night*, which he deeply believed in, was dead on arrival at theaters. Almost every top-earning actor or movie producer has flops and failures and downs as well as ups. If you can find the made-for-cable autobiographical films *His Way*, by and about Jerry Weintraub, and *A Piece of Work*, about Joan Rivers, I urge getting them and viewing them for raw, candid, dramatic demonstrations of rise, fall, and rise again.

Sinatra was once dropped by his record label, judged "washed up." Disneyland's live-televised grand opening was a comedy of errors, reported on by media as "a disaster", "not ready for prime time" and a place "not worth paying to visit." Ouch. And ouch again.

If you aren't willing to risk actions that may cause you personal, financial, or other embarrassment, you aren't going to be taking much action at all. So go ahead: screw up, fall down, embarrass yourself, and do a lot of it, as quickly as you can. Learn as much as you possibly can as you go. But, whatever you do, don't let yourself be imprisoned by the fear of making mistakes.

DEATH OF AN ACTOR

One of the saddest stories ever to come out of Hollywood was the rather sordid tale of the death of a young actor named Barry Brown. He played leading roles in *Bad Company* and *Daisy Miller*, and he was an actor of unusual promise. But he had the misfortune to do his best work in movies that were, in one way or another, unsuccessful. As he found it increasingly difficult to get parts, he became depressed, began drinking heavily and behaving erratically. He was found in his home, shot thorough the head with a gun and bottle beside him, and friends theorized he had been playing Russian roulette and had not intended suicide.

Barry Brown, dead at 27, had talent, looks, and intelligence. All he lacked was the one quality that, if absent, can make the rest useless: he lacked the ability to hang in, the emotional strength necessary to reject rejection and keep coming back for more.

It is the same in many professions, of course. "From salesman to saxophonist, the individual who risks something of himself in performance has to be somewhat inured to rebuff."

So wrote Bruce Cook, contributing editor to *American Film* magazine, in an article for *The Wall Street Journal* a few years ago.

This story is all the more tragic when you consider that it must be representative of tens of thousands of similar stories, some reported, some not, of people who gave up.

It's such stories that prove that talent, genius, and education are no assurances of success. In fact, the history of American business is full of stories of people lacking in those qualities but strong in persistence who have achieved the incredible.

One has to wonder how much greater America would be as a nation, in all respects, if the best and the brightest were also the most persistent.

Probably the best thing about being in business for yourself is that there isn't anybody to give a letter of resignation to when the going gets tough. Industrialist C.F. Kettering said, "No one ever would have crossed the ocean if he could have gotten off the ship in the storm."

I can think of a number of times when I've wanted to quit and didn't, mostly because I couldn't.

In my experience, far more business success comes purely from persistence than from invention or investment. There's a lot to be said for simply not giving up.

(*Note: Portions of the above reprinted from the book* Kennedy On Money/Business/Success, © 1985.)

So, How Do You Convert Failure to Success?

First, just by hanging in. Quite often, failure transforms itself to success purely as a result of persistence. Ernest Hemingway reportedly rewrote *The Old Man and the Sea* two hundred times and tried forty-four different endings for *A Farewell to Arms*. Keep trying a slightly different approach. But keep trying.

The insightful writer Ben Stein says, "Failure is like a patient teacher who tells us, 'No, *that* won't work. Try it a little differently. Or maybe a lot differently.' If you look at failure as a coach, as a manager encouraging you to try different approaches, you get a much better idea of what failure is."

Second, by diligently looking for the concealed opportunity. To quote proverbs and adages: nothing is either as good or as bad as it fist appears to be....and....whenever one door closes, another opens. Personally, every great disaster, disappointment, and tragedy in my life has directly led to a greater opportunity or benefit. Every single time. But you can only find what you look for, see what you expect to see.

Are there exceptions? I suppose so. There *are* some failures in which I've been unable to uncover any *immediate* benefit or opportunity – and those, set aside as "unfinished business" (rather than "permanent failure") have, in time, yielded enormous value. But these exceptions are few and far between.

Third, by taking prompt, decisive, constructive action. Stopping is the absolute worst thing that you can do. I wonder how many shots Michael Jordan *missed* (failures!) in his pro basketball career? Even how many *crucial* shots he missed? Well, one thing's certain; when he did miss one, he didn't rush over to the bench, get the coach to take him out of the game, sit down on the bench, put a towel over his head, and refuse to take another shot for the rest of the game. What did he do when he missed? As soon as possible, he took another shot. Cotton Fitzsimmons, a wise, veteran coach, now in management with the Phoenix Suns, says "Sometimes you have to let a player just shoot his way out of a slump." No, stopping is not the answer. Instead, as with most problems, action is the only true antidote.

EPILOGUE

By now, you should have "locked in" on the Ultimate Success Secret presented to you a number of times throughout this book. The people who are *living* this secret are the most respected and admired, influential and powerful, successful and happy individuals on the planet.

I would like to add a very brief discussion about just one application of this secret – and to quickly note that, like all advice, it's easier said than done; that, like "the fat doctor", I could stand to take my own medicine more frequently; but that does not diminish the importance of the ideas.

On the long, often dangerously boring drive from Phoenix to Las Vegas, there are signs posted frequently, at sites of deadly accidents, warning drivers not to drive if they've been drinking, not to drive if fatigued. The signs say:

There Is A LAST Time For Everything.

Tell your wife (or husband) you love her (or him) more often. And especially tell her (or him) today, because they might be gone tomorrow. There is a last time for everything.

Stop and have a friendly conversation with your Mom, Dad, a friend, the guy at the newsstand on the corner. Take just a few minutes for this more often than you do. And, especially today. They might be gone tomorrow. There is a last time for everything.

I called to talk to a friend the other day, another entrepreneur as busy, as obsessed as I; she wasn't in; when she called back she said, almost apologetically, and wryly, "I was out having a life." She had gone out to lunch with someone 100% unrelated to her business. Whatever it is that you really, really enjoy doing, really, really, really enjoy it the next time you do it. There is a last time for everything.

When you go to your job or place of business today, be thankful you've got one, and give it the very best you've got. Tomorrow, thousands will lose their jobs – and then, maybe, wish they'd done things there differently.

Tomorrow, a thousand entrepreneurs will close business doors – and then, maybe, wonder what might have happened if they'd advertised more creatively, sold more aggressively. There is a last time for everything.

Whatever you're going to do today, give it your best, and take from it the best you can. There is a last time for everything.

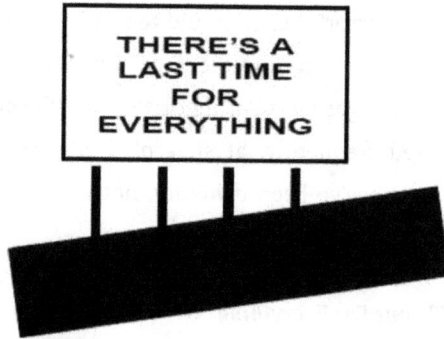

Just DO It. – Nike

25

Take Action to Make it All Happen

Dustin S. Burleson

THE REASON I get to stand up on stage before crowds of over 2,000 professionals and tell my story is that I have made more mistakes than all of you. Combined. I know you find that surprising, but it is the truth. Anyone who is successful has arrived at that success through a series of failures. The only difference, what helped them finally reach that success or goal, is that they kept getting back up. They didn't give up. Neither did I.

The most successful people in my life I have modeled. I've copied them on numerous levels. There is nothing unique or original on my part, and a major secret in how they operate is all in how they handle life's setbacks.

HANDLING FAILURE

On the delivery or discovery of "bad news" or "failure" they allow themselves minimal time in absorbing the failure, recognizing it, learning what they can from it, storing it away in their memory banks and getting back to work. Sure, failure at anything will feel like a blow to our ego and a setback. But it's all about how long you allow it to hold you back. Go ahead and feel the failure, for a brief time. Knowing what failure feels like should keep you persevering in order to succeed, because that feels so much better. You can't truly appreciate success unless you have experienced some failure to know what each feels like.

If there is a lawsuit, the death of a partner, loss of a major client, even bankruptcy, the best and most successful in our field allow themselves hours, or perhaps days, to be shocked, to be angry, to lament and fret, and they put it away and get back to work. Rather than choosing to be like most people and drop out of the game for weeks, months, years, or even quit for good, they push on, knowing that giving up will never help them reach their goals and will only leave them feeling empty, unfulfilled, and wishing they had stayed the course.

For the average person, a lawsuit, angry customer, an employee who steals, or the lost of trust from a partner would all be enough to make them drop out for weeks, months, years, or even quit for good. For many of these same people, just the thought of these "horrible failures" is more than enough to prevent them from ever taking the first steps to get started.

> *"Our greatest weakness lies in giving up. The most certain way to succeed is always to try just one more time." – Thomas Alva Edison*

FACING FEARS

Throughout your entire life, you have had to face fears in order to get to where you are today. When you were a toddler and wanted to take your first steps, you faced fears, and when you first wanted to ride a bike without training wheels, you had to face your fears. The thing is, most kids are not as afraid to face their fears as adults are. Kids will usually go for it; they will give it a shot and try it out. Sometimes they do it because they like the thrill of trying, sometimes they want the reward at the other end, and sometimes they just don't realize the size of the risk involved. But they take the risk and because they do, they keep going, persevering.

Somewhere along the way, adults become much more reserved about facing fears. They begin to worry about facing ridicule, being embarrassed, wasting their time, and so many other excuses that creep into their mind. But these fears begin to control us if we let them. That's when we will never reach the goals that we have set for ourselves. We cannot allow fear to hold us back and keep us from reaching the next level of success.

Do you have fears of failure that are keeping you from getting started on your next project or goal? How about fears that are keeping you from expanding your business? What about fears that are preventing you from hiring your next employee so that you can expand your services or from adding more hours to serve your clients better? How about fears of taking the leap to being the manager, visionary, and marketer of your thing and not the hourly employee who is tied to being the doer of your thing?

Think about what your fears are for a while. Nail them down. Once you know what they are, you can face them head on. Without facing those fears, you will never reach the level of success that you want. And here's the thing, you can successfully face those fears. The only thing that is holding you back from doing so is, well, you! If you could get out of your own way for just a little while, you will be able to overcome the challenges, learn from any failures, persevere, and go on to succeed.

Make no mistake, overcoming fears is not easy for everyone. I have had to overcome them in my life, just as anyone else who has succeeded. It may be hard work, it may take time, but if you want to succeed, it will be worth every effort you make.

"Setting goals is the first step in turning the invisible into the visible."
– Tony Robbins

Moving Forward, Making it Happen

By this point, you have taken in a great deal about how to take your practice to the next level. You have the information you need in order to turn your practice into the success that you have always wanted it to be. But only you can make it happen. In order to do that, you have to do what has been reiterated over and over throughout this book – take action.

As you finish this book, my hope is that you feel ready to take action. That you know what type of direction you want to go in and that you know how to make it happen. But most of all, that you realize that in order for anything to happen, you have to take action. You have to make it happen. What will you do first? Focus on escaping from your own personal prison, change your life, or leave behind excess baggage? Will you do what it takes to increase your salary, to win over worry, and to increase your profits? Do you know which one you should get started with first? If you were paying attention, you already know the answer to that question – all of them.

Get started by making a list of all the things you need to do in order to improve your practice and reach your goals. If, by chance, you finish this book and feel motivated to get started but are not sure how to start taking action, don't be afraid to reach out and take advantage of coaching. As a coach who has helped point over 1,600 orthodontists and dentists throughout seventeen countries in the right direction (the successful direction), I can help you as well. Sometimes working with someone who has been there and who has helped others can be an extremely effective way to get started.

Take the information you have learned throughout this book and put it to use. Don't just close the book, set it down, and move on to doing what you were doing when you first picked it up. You can do better than that. I challenge you to use this book as the springboard that takes you to the next phase of your business. Use this book to prompt you to take action.

ABOUT THE AUTHOR

Dr. Dustin S. Burleson is a speaker, teacher, author and business strategist for thousands of doctors located in eight different countries throughout the world. He writes and edits four newsletters monthly, is the director of the Rheam Foundation for Cleft & Craniofacial Orthodontics and operates a large multi-doctor, multi-clinic orthodontic and pediatric dental practice in Kansas City, Missouri. He is a champion of the private practitioner and has a long track record of helping orthodontists transform their practices and increase their impact on their families, employees, communities and the profession of orthodontics. His orthodontic marketing campaigns have generated over $300 million in revenue for his clients. When he is not working, you can find him on his sailboat, jumping out of airplanes, or racing exotic cars through the desert. In a tightly-contested vote, he was recently named Best Dad in the World by two-thirds of his children.

www.ingramcontent.com/pod-product-compliance
Lightning Source LLC
Chambersburg PA
CBHW030331220326
41518CB00048B/2229